SCHOLASTIC

Standardized Test Tutor

READING

Practice Tests With Question-by-Question Strategies and Tips That Help Students Build Test-Taking Skills and Boost Their Scores

Michael Priestley

Editor: Maria L. Chang
Cover design by Brian LaRossa
Interior design by Creative Pages, Inc.
Illustrations by Wilkinson Studios, Inc. and Creative Pages, Inc.
Photos: page 16 © Pictorial Press Ltd/Alamy; page 64 © Classic Image/Alamy

ISBN-13: 978-0-545-09604-1
ISBN-10: 0-545-09604-9
Copyright © 2009 by Michael Priestley
All rights reserved.
Printed in the U.S.A.

1   2   3   4   5   6   7   8   9   10   40   15 14 13 12 11 10 09

Contents

Answer Keys

Scoring Charts

Welcome to *Test Tutor*!

Students in schools today take a lot of tests, especially in reading and math. Some students naturally perform well on tests, and some do not. But just about everyone can get better at taking tests by learning more about what's on the test and how to answer the questions. How many students do you know who could benefit from working with a tutor? How many would love to have someone sit beside them and help them work their way through the tests they have to take?

That's where *Test Tutor* comes in. The main purpose of *Test Tutor* is to help students learn what they need to know in order to do better on tests. Along the way, *Test Tutor* will help students feel more confident as they come to understand the content and learn some of the secrets of success for multiple-choice tests.

The Test Tutor series includes books for reading and books for math in a range of grades. Each *Test Tutor* book in reading has three full-length practice tests designed specifically to resemble the state tests that students take each year. The reading skills measured on these practice tests have been selected from an analysis of the skills tested in ten major states, and the questions have been written to match the multiple-choice format used in most states.

The most important feature of this book is the friendly Test Tutor. He will help students work through the tests and achieve the kind of success they are looking for. This program is designed so students may work through the tests independently by reading the Test Tutor's helpful hints on the tests. Or you may work with the student as a tutor yourself, helping him or her understand each question and test-taking strategy along the way. You can do this most effectively by following the Test Tutor's guidelines included in the pages of this book.

Three Different Tests

There are three practice tests in this book: Test 1, Test 2, and Test 3. Each test has 40 multiple-choice items with four answer choices (A, B, C, D). All three tests measure the same skills, but they provide different levels of tutoring help.

Test 1 provides step-by-step guidance to help students find the answer to each question, as in the sample on the next page. The tips in Test 1 are detailed and thorough. Some of the tips are designed to help students read through and understand the passage, and others are written specifically for each reading question to help students figure out the answers.

Sample 1

Directions: Read this passage about a tryout for a game show. Then answer questions 1–6.

A Tough Decision

Yesterday, I let my best friend, Carla, beat me in a contest for the *Smart Aleck* game show. I hope I did the right thing. It was a tough decision, and I didn't have a lot of time to think about it. Here's what happened.

About a month ago, our principal, Mr. Gaudi, announced that our school had been selected to compete on *Smart Aleck*. Carla and I signed up right away because we both love *Smart Aleck*. We record it every day to watch when we get home. The game is like a trivia quiz. The questions are mostly serious, but there are a few where players have to answer a riddle or give the punch line to a joke. Carla has a good imagination, and I know a lot of history, so we figured we'd be good choices for the team.

> Think about who is telling this story and what she is worried about.

1. What is the main conflict in this passage?

   (A) The narrator is accused of cheating after she lets her friend win a contest.

   (B) Too many students sign up to be contestants on a game show.

   (C) The narrator has to decide whether to beat her best friend in a contest.

   (D) The principal and students disagree about choosing a game show team.

> Remember that a conflict is a problem that has to be solved.

Test 2 provides a test-taking tip for each item, as in the sample on the next page, but the tips are less detailed than in Test 1. They help guide the student toward the answers without giving away too much. Students must take a little more initiative.

Sample 2

Directions: Read this poem about houses. Then answer questions 13–18.

The House With Nobody in It

Whenever I walk to Suffern along the Erie track
I go by a poor old farmhouse with its shingles broken and black.
I suppose I've passed it a hundred times, but I always stop for a minute
And look at the house, the tragic house, the house with nobody in it.

I never have seen a haunted house, but I hear there are such things;   5
That they hold the talk of spirits, their mirth and sorrowings.
I know this house isn't haunted, and I wish it were, I do;
For it wouldn't be so lonely if it had a ghost or two.

> What is the speaker doing in this poem?

13. What is this poem mostly about?
- (A) a man and his wife
- (B) the road to Suffern
- (C) an old farmhouse
- (D) a gang of workmen

> Go back to the beginning of the poem to find the answer.

Test 3 does not provide test-taking tips. It assesses the progress students have made. After working through Tests 1 and 2 with the help of the Test Tutor, students should be more than ready to score well on Test 3 without too much assistance. Success on this test will help students feel confident and prepared for taking real tests.

Other Helpful Features

In addition to the tests, this book provides some other helpful features. First, on page 68, you will find an **answer sheet**. When students take the tests, they may mark their answers by filling in bubbles on the test pages. Or they may mark their answers on a copy of the answer sheet instead, as they will be required to do in most standardized tests. You may want to have students mark their answers on the test pages for Test 1 and then use an answer sheet for Tests 2 and 3 to help the student get used to filling in bubbles.

Second, beginning on page 69, you will find a detailed **answer key** for each test. The answer key lists the correct (and incorrect) responses and explains the answer for each question. It also identifies the skill tested by the question, as in the sample below.

Answer Key for Sample 1

Correct response: **C**
(*Analyze literary elements: plot*)
The narrator wonders whether she made the right decision, and the title refers to this same conflict.

Incorrect choices:

A The narrator wonders if she cheated, but no one accuses her of doing so.

B This is a smaller problem that is resolved with a playoff.

D The story says that "everybody" agreed this was a fair way to decide.

As the sample indicates, this question measures the student's ability to analyze the literary element of plot. This information can help you determine which skills the student has mastered and which ones still cause difficulty.

Finally, the answer key explains why each incorrect answer choice, or "distractor," is incorrect. This explanation can help reveal what error the student might have made. For example, a question about an effect might have a distractor that describes a cause instead. Knowing this could help the student improve his or her understanding of the text.

At the back of this book, you will find two scoring charts. The **Student Scoring Chart** helps you keep track of each student's scores on all three tests and on each passage (literary or informational). The **Classroom Scoring Chart** can be used to record the scores for all students on all three tests. This will help illustrate how much progress students have made from Test 1 to Test 3. Ideally, students should score higher on each test as they go through them. However, keep in mind that students get a lot of tutoring help on Test 1, some help on Test 2, and no help on Test 3. So if a student's scores on all three tests are fairly similar, that could still be a positive sign that the student is better able to read passages and answer comprehension questions independently and will achieve even greater success on future tests.

Read each passage and the questions that follow. Look at the Test Tutor's tips for understanding the passages and answering the questions. Then choose the best answer to each question.

Test Tutor says:

Directions: Read this passage about a tryout for a game show. Then answer questions 1–6.

A Tough Decision

Yesterday, I let my best friend, Carla, beat me in a contest for the *Smart Aleck* game show. I hope I did the right thing. It was a tough decision, and I didn't have a lot of time to think about it. Here's what happened.

About a month ago, our principal, Mr. Gaudi, announced that our school had been selected to compete on *Smart Aleck*. Carla and I signed up right away because we both love *Smart Aleck*. We record it every day to watch when we get home. The game is like a trivia quiz. The questions are mostly serious, but there are a few where players have to answer a riddle or give the punch line to a joke. Carla has a good imagination, and I know a lot of history, so we figured we'd be good choices for the team.

A few days after the announcement, Mr. Gaudi held a meeting in his office with everyone interested in being on the show. He reminded us that *Smart Aleck* uses a five-member team. He also said that three more people would be needed as backup in case one of the players got sick or something. Unfortunately, three times that many students had signed up. So Mr. Gaudi said we would have a playoff using practice questions, and the top eight scorers would become the team and the alternates. Everybody agreed that this was a fair way to decide.

Yesterday, all of the hopefuls gathered in the cafeteria after school. We drew numbers to decide the starting lineup and took our places. Mr. Gaudi acted as the moderator (which was sort of funny because he doesn't look anything like Bob Jansen, the real host of *Smart Aleck*). After a couple of hours, all the places on the team were

Think about who is telling this story and what she is worried about.

How did the principal choose the team?

Standardized Test Tutor: Reading (Grade 6) © 2009 by Michael Priestley, Scholastic Teaching Resources

set except one. Carla and I were tied for that last spot. We had to hold a one-on-one competition between the two of us. The winner would be on the team and the loser would be an alternate.

Midway through our two-person runoff, I was starting to pull ahead. Then I saw the look on Carla's face. I hesitated for a second but knew what I had to do. As much as I wanted to be a contestant on *Smart Aleck*, Carla wanted it even more. So, starting with my next question, I held back and let Carla win, just by a little bit. Her expression as she realized she would be on the show made up for my not being on the team. And since I will go as an alternate, I'll still have the fun of seeing the show up close.

What happens in the end?

Was I cheating by not trying as hard as I could? I don't think so. No one noticed, and Carla and I didn't plan it. It won't hurt the team because Carla will be a very good competitor on the real show. I think that making my best friend happy was the right thing to do.

Questions 1–6: Choose the best answer to each question.

1. What is the main conflict in this passage?

  Ⓐ The narrator is accused of cheating after she lets her friend win a contest.

  Ⓑ Too many students sign up to be contestants on a game show.

  Ⓒ The narrator has to decide whether to beat her best friend in a contest.

  Ⓓ The principal and students disagree about choosing a game show team.

Remember that a conflict is a problem that has to be solved.

2. What was the result of the meeting in Mr. Gaudi's office?

  Ⓐ The students prepared for the game show by answering special practice questions.

  Ⓑ Mr. Gaudi decided to hold a playoff to choose the team for the game show.

  Ⓒ The narrator and her friend Carla both signed up to be on *Smart Aleck*.

  Ⓓ Mr. Gaudi decided that the *Smart Aleck* team would have five members and three alternates.

Go back to the third paragraph to find the answer.

3. How are Carla and the narrator in this passage alike?

Ⓐ Each goes straight home after school to watch TV.

Ⓑ Both are good at making up jokes.

Ⓒ Each is willing to make sacrifices for the other.

Ⓓ Both are well qualified to be on the *Smart Aleck* team.

Check each answer choice against the passage to see if it is true.

4. The passage says, "Carla will be a very good *competitor* on the real show." What is the meaning of the word *competitor*?

Ⓐ a person who competes

Ⓑ not competing

Ⓒ a place where teams compete

Ⓓ before competing

Look at the parts of the word to figure out the meaning.

5. What happened after the students learned that too many kids wanted to participate?

Ⓐ The students gathered in the cafeteria for a playoff.

Ⓑ All interested students met in Mr. Gaudi's office.

Ⓒ The school was selected to compete on *Smart Aleck*.

Ⓓ The narrator and Carla signed up for the game show.

Look for signal words to figure out when events took place.

6. Which detail sentence would have to be omitted if this passage were rewritten from Carla's point of view?

Ⓐ We figured we'd be good choices for the team.

Ⓑ I hope I did the right thing.

Ⓒ Everybody agreed that this was a fair way to decide.

Ⓓ All the places on the team were set except one.

Put yourself in Carla's place and find the sentence that you would not say.

Standardized Test Tutor: Reading (Grade 6) © 2009 by Michael Priestley, Scholastic Teaching Resources

Directions: Read this article about chestnut trees. Then answer questions 7–12.

Where Have All the Chestnuts Gone?

Little more than a century ago, the American chestnut was one of the most important trees in the United States. It was also one of the most beautiful. This tree once made up 25 percent of the forests in the East. It covered millions of acres as far inland as Illinois. Today, it has almost vanished from the landscape.

Before 1900, there were so many American chestnuts that people said a squirrel could travel from Maine to Georgia by jumping from one to another without ever touching the ground. When chestnuts flowered in the spring, the white blossoms looked like snow on the mountains. These lovely trees grew large—up to 100 feet tall and four feet in diameter. Just one tree could yield enough boards to fill a railroad car.

Entire communities depended on the chestnut for daily life and as a source of income. Its wood was light, strong, easy to work with, and rot-resistant. So it was used for everything from houses to musical instruments. Native American medicine and folk remedies were made with the bark, leaves, and other parts of the tree. The bark was also used for tanning leather. The nuts made good food for people, livestock, and wildlife. They were also gathered and sold as a cash crop—again, filling up train cars headed for the cities. (For many years, roasted chestnuts were a tasty winter treat during the holidays.) The branches of the chestnut provided welcome shade in the summer. It was a marvelous tree.

Yes, it *was*. In the early 1900s, people began to notice that the trees were dying. A fungus had arrived from Asia on a different kind of chestnut tree. It infected mature American chestnuts, which had no immunity to the disease. The chestnut blight spread so fast that huge numbers of trees were killed before anyone fully realized what was happening.

> Take a quick look at the questions before you begin reading so you know what to look for.

> Why were chestnut trees so important?

The American chestnut is not extinct. The fungus does not kill the roots, which can still send up sprouts. However, as the sprouts grow, they too become infected and die back. Thus, the trees can never grow as large as they once did. Mature American chestnut trees are extremely rare.

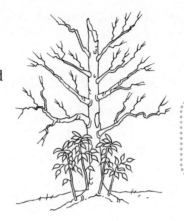

Still, all hope is not lost. Scientists are working to find a way to help the trees resist the fungus. Several national groups support this research. They also encourage the planting of American chestnuts so there will be plenty of trees still around when the blight is eventually conquered. Someday maybe people will once again see the "spring snow" of chestnut blossoms in the mountains. And squirrels will resume their treetop journeys from Maine to Georgia.

> Look at both pictures to help understand this part of the article.

> Think about the author's conclusion to the article.

Questions 7–12: Choose the best answer to each question.

7. What is the main idea of this article?

Ⓐ Chestnut trees may someday be saved by the efforts of researchers and others.

Ⓑ The American chestnut was struck by a powerful and fast-spreading fungus.

Ⓒ Chestnut trees flourished from Maine to Georgia and from the East Coast to Illinois.

Ⓓ The American chestnut was a beautiful and important tree that is now almost gone.

> Go back to the first paragraph of the article to find the main idea.

8. Comparing the two pictures in this article is most useful in helping the reader to—

Ⓐ visualize what an American chestnut looked like before and after the blight.

Ⓑ estimate how much shade a mature American chestnut could provide.

Ⓒ understand why American chestnut trees were infected by the blight.

Ⓓ explain how a blighted American chestnut sends up new sprouts.

> Look at the pictures again to see what information they provide.

Standardized Test Tutor: Reading (Grade 6) © 2009 by Michael Priestley, Scholastic Teaching Resources

9. What most likely happened as a result of the American chestnut blight?

Ⓐ Native Americans stopped using tree bark and leaves in folk medicines.

Ⓑ Communities that relied on chestnut trees suffered great hardships.

Ⓒ Other kinds of chestnut trees in the United States also began dying.

Ⓓ Landowners planted more American chestnut trees than in earlier years.

> Check each answer against the third paragraph to find the most likely result.

10. Which sentence from the article states an opinion?

Ⓐ For many years, roasted chestnuts were a tasty winter treat during the holidays.

Ⓑ Just one tree could yield enough boards to fill a railroad car.

Ⓒ Entire communities depended on the chestnut for daily life and as a source of income.

Ⓓ Its wood was light, strong, easy to work with, and rot-resistant.

> Remember that an opinion is a personal view or feeling that cannot be proven true.

11. Which detail from the article supports the idea that American chestnuts often grew close together?

Ⓐ The forests covered millions of acres.

Ⓑ Some trees measured four feet in diameter.

Ⓒ Squirrels could jump from one tree to another.

Ⓓ The trees were good for shade in the summer.

> Find the answer choice that would *not* be possible unless the trees grew close together.

12. The author organized the information in this article mainly by—

Ⓐ comparing life before and after the blight.

Ⓑ tracing the spread of the chestnut blight from Asia to the United States.

Ⓒ identifying the causes and effects of the chestnut blight.

Ⓓ describing events in chronological order.

> Look at the article as a whole to see how it presents information, from beginning to end.

Test Tutor says:

Directions: Read these two poems by Max Eastman. Then answer questions 13–18.

At the Aquarium

Serene the silver fishes glide,
Stern-lipped, and pale, and wonder-eyed!
As through the aged deeps of ocean,
They glide with wan and wavy motion.
They have no pathway where they go,   5
They flow like water to and fro.
They watch with never winking eyes,
They watch with staring, cold surprise,
The level people in the air,
The people peering, peering there: 10
Who wander also to and fro,
And know not why or where they go,
Yet have a wonder in their eyes,
Sometimes a pale and cold surprise.

—*Max Eastman*

> What is happening in this poem?

> What change takes place in this part of the poem?

In March

On a soaked fence-post a little blue-backed bird,
Opening her sweet throat, has stirred
A million music-ripples in the air
That curl and circle everywhere.
They break not shallow at my ear,   5
But quiver far within. Warm days are near!

—*Max Eastman*

> What is the speaker doing in this poem?

Questions 13–18: Choose the best answer to each question.

13. Between lines 6 and 8 in "At the Aquarium," the point of view changes from watching fish to—

Ⓐ staring at the water.

Ⓑ watching people.

Ⓒ staring in a mirror.

Ⓓ watching stars.

> Check each answer choice by going back to the poem.

Standardized Test Tutor: Reading (Grade 6) © 2009 by Michael Priestley, Scholastic Teaching Resources

14. In "At the Aquarium," what does the speaker suggest about people and fish?

Ⓐ They can never truly understand each other.

Ⓑ People sometimes behave as aimlessly as fish.

Ⓒ Fish and people are both suited to their environments.

Ⓓ People are more interesting to watch.

> Compare the speaker's description of the fish with his description of the people.

15. In the second poem, the poet compares the bird's song to—

Ⓐ a warm day.

Ⓑ bright colors.

Ⓒ the bird herself.

Ⓓ moving water.

> Look for clues in lines 3–5.

16. What is the second poem mostly about?

Ⓐ the need for fences

Ⓑ a million sounds

Ⓒ the coming of spring

Ⓓ a broken heart

> Read the ending of the poem again to decide.

17. Which line includes an example of alliteration?

Ⓐ Serene the silver fishes glide,

Ⓑ They have no pathway where they go,

Ⓒ The level people in the air,

Ⓓ That curl and circle everywhere.

> Look for two or more words in a line that begin with the same sound.

18. What do these two poems have in common?

Ⓐ They use similar images to express ideas.

Ⓑ They convey the same mood.

Ⓒ They use the same rhyming pattern.

Ⓓ They are both examples of free verse.

> Check each answer choice to see which one is true.

Directions: Read this passage about Charles Dickens. Then answer questions 19–25.

A Story of Hope

By 1843, English author Charles Dickens had already written eight novels, but he was broke. He needed money to support his family. So he dashed off a slim volume called *A Christmas Carol*. It told the story of a man named Ebenezer Scrooge. The first 6,000 copies of the book sold out in a week. But even this early success could not have

A scene from *A Christmas Carol*

> Scan the questions before you read the passage so you know what to look for.

predicted the life Scrooge would go on to lead. At the time, motion pictures had not yet been invented. But Ebenezer Scrooge would one day become a film and stage star.

Never out of print in 165 years, *A Christmas Carol* has inspired countless stage versions. The first play was overseen by Dickens himself in 1844. The first two movie versions were silent films in 1901 and 1908. Since then, the story has been remade more than 60 times for television and cinema. In fact, many people know the story without ever having read the book.

What makes this tale so appealing? Audiences have always loved a good plot, a good villain, and the triumph of right over wrong. *A Christmas Carol* offers all three.

> Think about why the story is so popular.

Ebenezer Scrooge is a terrific villain. A heartless miser, he lives alone in a dreary house. In the opening scenes, he is harsh with his clerk and turns away his only living relative. When asked for money to help the needy, he points out that his taxes already pay for workhouses. (These were grim places where the homeless of the time were sent.) As Scrooge sits down to his evening meal, the ghost of his late partner appears. Jacob Marley tells Scrooge that he is on the path to ruin. But he has the chance to turn his life around.

During the night, Scrooge is visited by three spirits. The first reveals scenes from Scrooge's youth that led to his current state. The second takes him to the homes of his clerk and his nephew. Here Scrooge sees that people can be happy without a lot of money.

Standardized Test Tutor: Reading (Grade 6) © 2009 by Michael Priestley, Scholastic Teaching Resources

The spirit also shows him the desperate poor people of London, whose lives he has dismissed so coldly. The final spirit shows Scrooge what will become of him if he continues to live as he has. He will die alone, and no one will care. At last the message sinks in, and Scrooge repents. He becomes a new person. He is generous and caring to all around him, especially to his clerk's sickly son, Tiny Tim.

Over the years, many thespians have played the role of Scrooge. Who wouldn't enjoy playing such a character? Actors as varied as Shakespearean player Sir Derek Jacobi, *Star Trek* cast member Patrick Stewart, and cartoon character Mister Magoo have all played Ebenezer.

Every year, many thousands of people tune in to watch *A Christmas Carol* once again. Why? They may be touched by its lessons on the true meanings of wealth and happiness. They may enjoy the special effects, or watching every year may be just a habit. The answer most likely lies in the unforgettable Ebenezer Scrooge, both villain and hero. Viewers never seem to grow tired of the old miser and his dramatic message of hope and change.

> How does Scrooge change during the story?

Questions 19–25: Choose the best answer to each question.

19. What is the main idea of this passage?

Ⓐ Charles Dickens needed money for his family.

Ⓑ Many who have not read *A Christmas Carol* still know the story.

Ⓒ *A Christmas Carol* is a story set in England.

Ⓓ The story of Ebenezer Scrooge has become popular on screen and stage.

> Go back to the first paragraph to find the main idea.

20. Which detail is not essential to the main idea and could have been left out?

Ⓐ The book has never been out of print in 165 years.

Ⓑ Charles Dickens wrote *A Christmas Carol* in 1843.

Ⓒ The first play was overseen by Dickens himself in 1844.

Ⓓ Every year, thousands of people watch *A Christmas Carol* again.

> Check each answer choice to see if it supports the main idea.

21. The use of the phrase *dashed off* in the third sentence of the passage suggests that Dickens—

Ⓐ destroyed the book.   Ⓒ wrote the book in a hurry.

Ⓑ ran home to start writing.   Ⓓ had poor handwriting.

> Read the first few sentences of the passage to look for clues.

22. According to this passage, what did Ebenezer Scrooge do last?

Ⓐ He visited the home of his nephew.

Ⓑ He saw some poor people living in London.

Ⓒ He became generous and caring.

Ⓓ He received a warning from Jacob Marley.

> Go back to the fifth paragraph to see what he did.

23. Which detail best supports the idea that Charles Dickens was a popular writer before he wrote *A Christmas Carol*?

Ⓐ He staged a play based on the book.

Ⓑ The book sold 6,000 copies in a week.

Ⓒ He is described as the "English author."

Ⓓ The book has never gone out of print.

> Read each answer carefully to see if it shows that Dickens was popular.

24. The passage says, "Over the years, many *thespians* have played the role of Scrooge." What are *thespians*?

Ⓐ actors   Ⓒ writers

Ⓑ evil villains   Ⓓ lonely people

> Look for clues in the sentences before and after the word.

25. Which is the best summary of this passage?

Ⓐ Charles Dickens wrote *A Christmas Carol* in 1843. He needed money to support his family.

Ⓑ Ebenezer Scrooge is the main character in Charles Dickens's book *A Christmas Carol*. The story has been remade many times for stage and screen.

Ⓒ Charles Dickens wrote *A Christmas Carol* when his family needed money. The book sold out in a week and has never been out of print.

Ⓓ People love *A Christmas Carol* because of its colorful characters. The movie has been remade more than 60 times.

> Find the answer that tells about the whole passage.

Standardized Test Tutor: Reading (Grade 6) © 2009 by Michael Priestley, Scholastic Teaching Resources

Test Tutor says:

Directions: Read this passage about a boy who catches a mouse. Then answer questions 26–32.

The Silver Mouse

Once upon a time on his way to the playground, a boy named Gregory caught a tiny silver-colored mouse outside his apartment building. While he was pondering what to do with it, the mouse spoke to him. "Oh, most benevolent human," it pleaded, "please do not hurt me. I am no ordinary mouse. If you release me, I can be of great service to you."

Gregory did not see how a talking mouse could help him. But the creature's anxious look persuaded him to let it go anyway. He set the mouse unharmed on the sidewalk and started toward the corner.

"Wait," called the mouse, "don't you want to ask for something?"

Gregory thought for a moment and said, "How about a high-definition TV?" He never believed for a minute that the mouse could fulfill such a request. But when he got home after his basketball game, he found his mother in a state of excitement. There in the living room in a carton labeled "Silvermouse Enterprises" was a 42-inch HD television.

When Gregory explained to his astonished mother what had happened, she couldn't believe her ears. "You had a magic mouse under your thumb and all you asked for was a TV?" she exclaimed. "Why, you could have asked for a house! Go find the mouse and ask for a house. I want a really big house in the suburbs."

Although it seemed like a lot to ask for, Gregory reluctantly went outside. Standing in the same place as before, he chanted, "*Oh, Silver Mouse, Silver Mouse, my mother wants you to help us out.*"

Gregory heard a scurrying sound, and the mouse appeared. "Did you like the TV?" Gregory said that the television was far better than he had expected. Then, somewhat embarrassed, he relayed his mother's wish.

"She shall have her house immediately," declared the mouse.

Sure enough, Gregory returned home to find his mother oohing and ahing at pictures of a fancy new house. Gregory wasn't convinced he wanted to live in the suburbs, but he said nothing. His mother seemed so delighted that he couldn't bear to disappoint her. However, as they drove to their new neighborhood the next day, he was already starting to miss his buddies. There were no basketball hoops anywhere.

What kind of passage begins like this?

What did the mouse do for Gregory?

How is Gregory different from his mother?

After about a month in their new house, Gregory's mother started to complain that the house was too hard to take care of. "Go tell that mouse we need a maid, a cook, and a gardener," she ordered. Gregory protested, but his mother insisted.

So that Saturday, he took the train into the city. Walking through his old neighborhood, he gazed wistfully at the kids playing basketball in the park. When he reached his old building, he chanted, "*Oh, Silver Mouse, Silver Mouse, my mother wants you to help us out.*" He heard a scurrying sound, and the mouse appeared.

"Let me guess," said the mouse. "Your mother isn't satisfied with her house." Hanging his head, Gregory admitted that his mother now wanted servants. "She shall have them immediately," declared the mouse. Then it disappeared through the fence.

Gregory made the long trip home and discovered that, once again, the mouse had delivered on its promise.

Several months went by before Gregory's mother again grew discontent. "The weather around here is terrible," she grumbled. "I want a new climate that is never too hot, too cold, too wet, or too dry. Better yet, I want to be in charge of the weather. Then I can change conditions to suit my mood. Go and tell the rodent of my wishes."

Gregory sighed and headed into the city once again. He chanted, "*Oh, Silver Mouse, Silver Mouse, my mother wants you to help us out.*"

With a scurrying sound, the mouse appeared. "What now?" asked the mouse. When Gregory told him, the mouse replied, "She shall have her climate change immediately."

In the very next moment, a yellow taxicab pulled up at the curb. Gregory's mother was in the back seat. The driver unloaded a large number of boxes and suitcases onto the sidewalk. As he drove away, the mouse climbed atop the mountain of luggage and addressed Gregory's mother.

"Too bad for you," it scolded. "You could have had anything within reason. But instead, your greediness has returned you to where you started. I certainly hope you enjoy city weather!"

As the mouse disappeared through the fence, Gregory and his mother started to lug their belongings up the stairs. Upon entering their old apartment, Gregory smiled to himself. The HD television was gone, but there in the middle of the carpet were a brand new basketball and a pair of the latest basketball shoes.

Gregory never saw the silver mouse again.

> Notice how many things the mother asks for.

> Think about what happens at the end. Did you know this would happen?

Standardized Test Tutor: Reading (Grade 6) © 2009 by Michael Priestley, Scholastic Teaching Resources

Questions 26–32: Choose the best answer to each question.

26. "The Silver Mouse" is most like what kind of literature?

    Ⓐ essay   Ⓒ folktale

    Ⓑ science fiction   Ⓓ biography

    > Think of what you know about each kind of literature.

27. Why did Gregory let the mouse go at the beginning?

    Ⓐ He felt sorry for it.   Ⓒ He was in a hurry.

    Ⓑ The mouse bit him.   Ⓓ The mouse granted his wish.

    > Check the second paragraph to find the answer.

28. That Gregory had the mouse "under his thumb" means he—

    Ⓐ gave the mouse a thumbs-up sign.

    Ⓑ caught the mouse with his thumb.

    Ⓒ had control of the mouse.

    Ⓓ squeezed the mouse in his hand.

    > Look at the fifth paragraph to see what this phrase means.

29. Why was Gregory reluctant to tell the mouse his mother's requests?

    Ⓐ He was afraid his friends would see him talking to a mouse.

    Ⓑ He believed that she was asking for too much.

    Ⓒ He thought the mouse might not respond.

    Ⓓ He did not want to move out of the neighborhood.

    > Go back to the sixth paragraph to see why he was reluctant.

30. As the story goes along, how can you tell that the mouse is losing patience?

    Ⓐ It argues with Gregory about his mother's wishes.

    Ⓑ It takes longer to arrive each time Gregory calls.

    Ⓒ The look on its face shows how it feels.

    Ⓓ It sounds more annoyed each time it appears.

    > You can tell a lot from what a character says and does.

31. Which detail is the best clue that this story takes place in the very recent past?

(A) a high-definition TV   (C) a playground

(B) the silver mouse   (D) boxes and suitcases

Look at each answer choice before you pick one.

32. Which saying best expresses a theme of this story?

(A) Getting up early makes a man wise.

(B) Make the best of what you've got.

(C) Home is where you hang your hat.

(D) A small leak will sink a great ship.

Remember that the theme is the message, or lesson, the author wants you to learn.

Standardized Test Tutor: Reading (Grade 6) © 2009 by Michael Priestley, Scholastic Teaching Resources

Directions: Read these two passages about donating blood. Then answer questions 33–40.

Passage 1: So You Want to Donate Blood

Why Donating Blood Is Important

Did you know that every two seconds in America, someone in a hospital needs blood? There are several reasons for needing blood. People get in an accident, have an operation, or develop certain kinds of diseases. If they cannot get a transfusion, they may get sicker or even die. Donating blood saves lives!

Who, Where, and How

Almost anyone can donate blood. According to the American Red Cross, donors must be at least 17 years old (16 in some states). They must weigh at least 110 pounds. They must be healthy. They must not have given blood in the last eight weeks.

Donating blood is very safe for most people. To be sure it is safe for you, a nurse or medical person will start by asking some questions. Then he or she will check your temperature and blood pressure and test a drop of your blood.

Donating blood is simple. To start with, you have to find a blood donation center or blood drive. The Red Cross has Web sites that list places and times to give blood. Most towns and cities post announcements about upcoming blood drives.

At most blood drives, you start by signing in and getting a number. You go through the medical check-in and then wait your turn. When your number is called, you go and sit or lie on a cot with your arm on a special support. Then a phlebotomist, whose specialty is collecting blood, puts a rubber strap around your arm and gives you a rubber ball to squeeze. (This is to make your veins stand out so they are easier to find.) The person slips a needle into a vein and then loosens the band. This allows your blood to flow freely through the needle. From there it goes into a tube and into a collection bag.

After about ten minutes, the person disconnects the bag and puts a bandage on your arm. At this point, you might feel a little light-headed. When you are ready, a volunteer walks you over to a table for some juice and snacks like cookies, pretzels, or raisins. It is especially important to drink lots of liquid to replace what you just

Take a quick look at both passages and the questions so you know what to expect.

What is this passage mostly about?

How do people give blood?

Standardized Test Tutor: Reading (Grade 6) © 2009 by Michael Priestley, Scholastic Teaching Resources

gave away. The snacks may seem like the best thing about donating blood. But the real best thing is knowing that your pint of blood may save someone's life.

Where Does Donated Blood Go?

You've probably heard of "blood banks." These are special places where blood is stored until it is needed. Blood must be stored at exactly the right temperature. It must also be handled very carefully to prevent infections. The blood banks test each donated unit to be sure it is free from viruses and other problems. Then they separate the blood into three parts: red cells (which can be kept for up to 42 days), plasma (one year), and platelets (five days). This means that each unit could help up to three people.

Most hospitals keep a supply of blood on hand. But they can also contact the blood centers 24 hours a day if they run out or need a certain type. Especially when the needed type is rare, the centers contact one another to find a source. A computer system is used to keep track of the national blood supply. Hospitals use more than 29 million units of blood every year.

Never Too Young to Help

Even those who are too young to donate blood themselves can still help. Most blood drives need volunteers to put up posters. They need people to give out cookies and juice, and even keep donors company while they wait. Young people can also tell their parents and other adults how blood donation works and how important it is.

Think about what you have learned from this passage.

Standardized Test Tutor: Reading (Grade 6) © 2009 by Michael Priestley, Scholastic Teaching Resources

Passage 2:
Student Council Holds Blood Drive

The Westwood Middle School Student Council has decided to hold a blood drive, and you can help.

HELP WITH THE BLOOD DRIVE!	How You Can Help
The Student Council is holding a blood drive for teachers, parents, and townspeople. We need everyone's help to make this drive a success. That includes *you*! Our goal is to collect 50 units of blood. That means we need to have at least 65 people come to the drive. Pick up information brochures from the office or get them from any Student Council member. Pass them out to any adults you know. Even your older siblings and their friends can donate if they are healthy and at least 17 years old. The blood drive will take place on Tuesday, October 21, from 3:00 to 6:00 P.M., in the cafeteria. Free babysitting for donors' children will be provided during those hours.	There are lots of ways to help. The most important is to find donors, so talk to people! Here are some other things you can do: • Put up posters around town. • Make cookies for snacks. • Plan games and other entertainment for the babysitting center. • Volunteer for a babysitting shift. • Greet donors at the school entrance and tell them where the cafeteria is. • Visit with donors while they wait. • Make "Thank You" cards to give to everyone who donates. **Remember—every pint of blood can help save as many as three lives!**

What kind of passage is this?

How can this chart help you?

Questions 33–40: Choose the best answer to each question.

For each question, decide which passage it refers to.

33. Passage 1 says, "If they cannot get a *transfusion*, they may get sicker or even die." The word *transfusion* means—

    Ⓐ "medical attention."

    Ⓑ "transportation to a hospital."

    Ⓒ "the name of a doctor."

    Ⓓ "a transfer of blood."

Go back to the first paragraph to look for clues.

34. Under which heading in Passage 1 should you look for information about how blood banks store pints of blood?

Ⓐ **Why Donating Blood Is Important**

Ⓑ **Who, Where, and How**

Ⓒ **Where Does Donated Blood Go?**

Ⓓ **Never Too Young to Help**

> Skim each section to see what it tells about.

35. When giving blood, what is the effect of tightening a rubber strap around a blood donor's arm?

Ⓐ Blood flows freely into the collection bag.

Ⓑ The donor feels light-headed.

Ⓒ Blood vessels in the donor's arm stand out.

Ⓓ The donor is able to squeeze a rubber ball.

> Review the fifth paragraph to find the answer.

36. The main purpose of Passage 2 is to—

Ⓐ help students stay healthy.

Ⓑ persuade students to help with the blood drive.

Ⓒ tell an entertaining story about a school blood drive.

Ⓓ give information about donating blood.

> Think about why the author wrote this passage.

37. If you were trying to recruit donors for a blood drive at your school, reading Passage 1 would help you most by—

Ⓐ supplying information to help you answer questions.

Ⓑ explaining where to find a blood bank.

Ⓒ suggesting ways to entertain the donors' children.

Ⓓ identifying the best kind of snacks to make for the donors.

> Check each answer choice to see which one makes the most sense.

Standardized Test Tutor: Reading (Grade 6) © 2009 by Michael Priestley, Scholastic Teaching Resources

38. Passage 2 mentions volunteering for "a babysitting *shift*." What meaning of the word *shift* best fits in this sentence?

Ⓐ a change from one place to another

Ⓑ a straight, loose-fitting dress

Ⓒ a handle used to change gears in a car or truck

Ⓓ a person's scheduled period of work

Try each answer choice in the sentence to see which one fits.

39. The Student Council's goal is to collect 50 units of blood. What is the most likely reason they want 65 people to come to the drive?

Ⓐ Some of the donors might not feel well after giving their blood.

Ⓑ Some people do not like the idea of giving blood.

Ⓒ Some blood might be lost or spilled on the way to the hospital.

Ⓓ Some people who show up may not be qualified to give blood.

Go back to Passage 1 to see what kinds of people can give blood.

40. How do these two passages compare as sources of information?

Ⓐ Both identify ways that young people can help with blood drives.

Ⓑ The information in Passage 1 is more useful to students.

Ⓒ Both give detailed information about the blood donation process.

Ⓓ Passage 2 tries harder to encourage people to give blood.

Read each answer choice to find the one that sounds right.

End of Test 1 **STOP**

Standardized Test Tutor: Reading (Grade 6) © 2009 by Michael Priestley, Scholastic Teaching Resources

Read each passage and the questions that follow. Look at the Test Tutor's tips for understanding the passages and answering the questions. Then choose the best answer to each question.

Test Tutor says:

Directions: Read this passage about two Native American tribes in the Pacific Northwest. Then answer questions 1–6.

The Bridge of the Gods

A long time ago, the Multnomahs and Klickitats were two neighboring tribes that had fallen on hard times. Wy'East was chief of the Multnomahs, and Klickitat was chief of his tribe. Together, the two chiefs prayed to the Great Spirit to help the people in their time of need. While the chiefs slept that night, the Great Spirit heard their prayers and whisked them to the Columbia River area, with its great forests and abundant game.

When the chiefs woke up, the Great Spirit made them face in opposite directions. Klickitat faced north and shot an arrow, and the place where his arrow landed marked the edge of his tribe's new land. Wy'East shot his arrow south over the Willamette River Valley, which became the Multnomahs' new homeland. Everyone was happy. The Great Spirit then built a sign of peace between the tribes: a bridge of land across the Columbia River, complete with tall trees and great big rocks. It was called the Bridge of the Gods.

For years the two tribes crossed the bridge often to hunt, fish, and trade together. Food was plentiful, and life grew comfortable for everyone. However, at that time no one on Earth had fire except for one old woman named Lewit, who lived alone high up in the mountains.

The Great Spirit asked the old woman, "What would it take for you to share your fire with others?"

Lewit answered, "I would share my fire if I could be young and beautiful again."

"If you take your fire to the Bridge of the Gods tomorrow morning, you will get your wish," said the Great Spirit.

Sure enough, the next morning a lovely young woman sat in front of her fire in the middle of the land bridge. The Klickitat and Multnomah people took fire home to heat their lodges. They used

> Look for details that tell where the story takes place and how it begins.

> Think about what the characters say and do.

fire to cook with and to light their homes at night. They were very pleased with Lewit's gift.

Wy'East and Klickitat were so pleased with the young woman that they both wanted to marry her. Wy'East brought her a gift. Then Klickitat brought her a bigger and better gift. The chiefs began to argue, and soon the tribes got involved, all fighting over which chief would marry Lewit.

The fighting angered the Great Spirit, who caused Earth to shake. Earth shook so much that the Bridge of the Gods collapsed into the river, but the Great Spirit was still angry. For punishment, he changed the two leaders and the woman into mountains that would never speak or move again. Wy'East was changed into Mount Hood, Klickitat into Mount Adams, and Lewit into Mount St. Helens. And that is how these great mountains of the Pacific Northwest came to be.

> Think about what changes have taken place.

Questions 1–6: Choose the best answer to each question.

1. In this passage, why did the Great Spirit become angry?
   - Ⓐ Wy'East and Klickitat asked for the Great Spirit's help.
   - Ⓑ The tribes were fighting over who would marry Lewit.
   - Ⓒ Wy'East and Klickitat gave no thanks for the gift of fire.
   - Ⓓ The tribes did not respect the Bridge of the Gods.

> Look at the ending of the story to find the answer.

2. Which event happens first?
   - Ⓐ Lewit agrees to share her fire.
   - Ⓑ Klickitat brings a nice gift to Lewit.
   - Ⓒ Wy'East shoots an arrow to the south.
   - Ⓓ The Great Spirit creates the Bridge of the Gods.

> Go back to the passage to find the answer.

3. Which words best describe the Great Spirit in this story?
   - Ⓐ *greedy* and *loving*
   - Ⓑ *fair* and *kindhearted*
   - Ⓒ *cold* and *distant*
   - Ⓓ *unjust* and *cruel*

> Think of this character as a real person. What is he like?

Test Tutor says:

4. What can you infer about the Multnomah and Klickitat tribes at the beginning of the story?

(A) Neither tribe used fire for cooking.

(B) They did not get along with each other.

(C) Both tribes lived happy, peaceful lives.

(D) They did not have anything to trade with each other.

> Check each answer against the beginning of the story.

5. The people moved "to the Columbia River area, with its great forests and abundant *game*." Which definition of *game* best fits in this sentence?

> **game** *noun* **1.** an amusement or pastime. **2.** a competitive activity involving skill or chance. **3.** a business or profession. **4.** wild animals that are hunted.

(A) definition 1

(B) definition 2

(C) definition 3

(D) definition 4

> Look for clues in the sentences before and after this word.

6. Which sentence best expresses a theme of this story?

(A) Be thankful for what you have.

(B) Things are not what they seem.

(C) Faith will move mountains.

(D) All things come to those who wait.

> Think about the lesson you can learn from what happens.

Standardized Test Tutor: Reading (Grade 6) © 2009 by Michael Priestley, Scholastic Teaching Resources

Directions: Read this passage about plastic. Then answer questions 7–12.

Wondrous, Dangerous Plastic

Today's world is full of plastic goods, from water bottles to car parts. We make plastic toys, toothbrushes, and shopping bags. Plastic is so useful that it's hard to imagine life without it, but it has not been around that long.

The first plastic was invented in 1869. That's when American John Wesley Hyatt made a form of plastic from a plant material called cellulose. Before long, his discovery was used to make combs, eyeglasses, buttons, and film.

In the 1900s, petroleum products such as oil replaced cellulose. New kinds of plastic were discovered in the 1950s, and that's when the real boom began. Plastic quickly replaced paper, glass, metal, and wood in a growing number of products. In 1960, the United States made 6 billion pounds of plastic. By 1988, the output had grown to 50 billion pounds. These days, almost 10 percent of the oil America uses every year is turned into plastic. That's 2 million barrels of oil a day.

Most of the plastic ever made still exists. Unlike wood, metal, and paper, plastic does not break down easily. Some people think plastic will never break down. Others say it may take 500 or 1,000 years. No one knows for sure because it has been around for too short a time. But if George Washington had used plastic water bottles in the 1700s, those bottles would probably still be around.

Although plastic lasts a long time, we don't keep plastic products very long. We use them and throw them away. Only about 5 percent of plastic is recycled. A huge amount of it ends up floating in the ocean. Then seabirds, seals, turtles, whales, and fish eat it. Scientists

Scan the questions before you start reading the passage.

Think about the title of the passage as you read.

often find sea animals that have starved to death with their stomachs full of plastic. And every time it rains, more trash from city streets flushes into the sea. Much of that trash is plastic.

What can we do about plastic? First, be aware. Oil takes millions of years to form. Should we use up this precious fuel to make flimsy shopping bags that are used once and thrown away? Should any animal pay for our convenience with its life? Each person's actions can make a difference. The time to act is now.

Ways to Reduce Plastic in the Environment
Limit the amount of plastic you buy. When you can, buy goods made from material that breaks down or can be recycled.
Instead of accepting a store's plastic bags to carry your purchases, shop with cloth bags that can be reused.
Use waxed paper for sandwiches instead of plastic wrap or sandwich bags.
Drink water from the tap rather than little plastic bottles.
Recycle all the plastic you can, including takeout food and drink containers.
Don't buy things packaged in lots of plastic.
Keep music players, computers, and cell phones rather than tossing them out for newer versions.
Write to makers of products you buy, asking them to reduce or avoid plastic packaging.
Don't litter. Make sure that any plastic you can't recycle or reuse goes into a trash can.

Why does the author include this chart?

Questions 7–12: Choose the best answer to each question.

7. Which is the best summary of the fourth paragraph?

Ⓐ Plastic takes longer to break down than other materials.

Ⓑ Scientists argue about how long plastic takes to break down.

Ⓒ George Washington's plastic water bottles will be here for at least 500 years.

Ⓓ Plastic may break down in 500 years, but it's too soon to tell for sure.

Go back to the fourth paragraph to see what it's about.

Test Tutor says:

8. The author's main purpose in this passage is to—

   Ⓐ explain how plastic is made.

   Ⓑ criticize those who make and buy plastic.

   Ⓒ compare plastic with other kinds of products.

   Ⓓ convince people to use less plastic.

> Think about why the author wrote this passage.

9. The passage says, "Should we use up this precious fuel to make *flimsy* shopping bags that are used once and thrown away?" The word *flimsy* suggests that—

   Ⓐ these bags are very useful.   Ⓒ these bags won't last long.

   Ⓑ oil is not really valuable.   Ⓓ oil is hard to find.

> Look for clues in the sentence to figure out the meaning of the word.

10. Which sentence from the passage best shows the author's bias?

   Ⓐ Plastic is so useful that it's hard to imagine life without it.

   Ⓑ Should any animal pay for our convenience with its life?

   Ⓒ Almost 10 percent of the oil America uses every year is turned into plastic.

   Ⓓ Most of the plastic ever made still exists.

> Read all of the answer choices carefully. Look for one that tells what the author feels.

11. Which of these is *not* a good way for people to reduce the amount of plastic in the environment?

   Ⓐ Use cloth shopping bags instead of disposable plastic ones.

   Ⓑ Hold onto plastic goods that still work, like cell phones, rather than buying new ones.

   Ⓒ Cut plastic into pieces before discarding so it breaks down faster.

   Ⓓ Drink tap water and avoid buying water in plastic bottles.

> Use the chart to figure out the answer.

12. Which detail supports the idea that plastic can be dangerous?

   Ⓐ Animals can starve to death after eating plastic.

   Ⓑ Plastic is an extremely useful material.

   Ⓒ About 10 percent of the oil we use every year is made into plastic.

   Ⓓ John Wesley Hyatt made the first plastic from cellulose.

> Find the detail that mentions something dangerous.

Standardized Test Tutor: Reading (Grade 6) © 2009 by Michael Priestley, Scholastic Teaching Resources

Directions: Read this poem about houses. Then answer questions 13–18.

The House With Nobody in It

Whenever I walk to Suffern along the Erie track
I go by a poor old farmhouse with its shingles broken and black.
I suppose I've passed it a hundred times, but I always stop for a minute
And look at the house, the tragic house, the house with nobody in it.

I never have seen a haunted house, but I hear there are such things;   5
That they hold the talk of spirits, their mirth and sorrowings.
I know this house isn't haunted, and I wish it were, I do;
For it wouldn't be so lonely if it had a ghost or two.

This house on the road to Suffern needs a dozen panes of glass,
And somebody ought to weed the walk and take a scythe to the grass.   10
It needs new paint and shingles, and the vines should be trimmed and tied;
But what it needs the most of all is some people living inside.

If I had a lot of money and all my debts were paid
I'd put a gang of men to work with brush and saw and spade.
I'd buy that place and fix it up the way it used to be   15
And I'd find some people who wanted a home and give it to them free.

Now, a new house standing empty, with staring windows and door,
Looks idle, perhaps, and foolish, like a hat on its block in the store.
But there's nothing mournful about it; it cannot be sad and lone
For the lack of something within it that it has never known.   20

But a house that has done what a house should do,
    a house that has sheltered life,
That has put its loving wooden arms around a man and his wife,
A house that has echoed a baby's laugh and held up his stumbling feet,
Is the saddest sight, when it's left alone, that ever your eyes could meet.   25

(continued)

> What is the speaker doing in this poem?

> What does the speaker say about houses?

Standardized Test Tutor: Reading (Grade 6) © 2009 by Michael Priestley, Scholastic Teaching Resources

So whenever I go to Suffern along the Erie track
I never go by the empty house without stopping and looking back,
Yet it hurts me to look at the crumbling roof and the shutters fallen apart,
For I can't help thinking the poor old house is a house with a broken heart.

—*Joyce Kilmer (1886–1918)*

> How does the speaker feel at the end?

Questions 13–18: Choose the best answer to each question.

13. What is this poem mostly about?

Ⓐ a man and his wife

Ⓑ the road to Suffern

Ⓒ an old farmhouse

Ⓓ a gang of workmen

> Go back to the beginning of the poem to find the answer.

14. What does the speaker in this poem suggest about houses?

Ⓐ Houses should have babies in them.

Ⓑ Once people live in a house, it becomes somehow human.

Ⓒ Sad old houses really should be taken down.

Ⓓ People have a responsibility to keep their houses clean and neat.

> Read the sixth stanza again.

15. In lines 17–20, the speaker compares a new but empty house to—

Ⓐ a broken heart.

Ⓑ a hat in a store.

Ⓒ wooden arms.

Ⓓ vines that need trimming.

> Read these lines again to find the answer.

16. Which sentence describes an important characteristic of this poem?

Ⓐ It has no regular rhythm.

Ⓑ It is written as a conversation.

Ⓒ It repeats the same lines many times.

Ⓓ It is written in couplets that rhyme.

> Check each answer choice against the poem to see which one is true.

17. From the first two lines of the poem, you can tell that the speaker is—

Ⓐ walking near a railroad.

Ⓑ living in a large city.

Ⓒ walking on an island.

Ⓓ living in a foreign country.

> Look for clues at the beginning of the poem.

18. What does the speaker reveal about his or her character in this poem?

Ⓐ restlessness

Ⓑ delight in life

Ⓒ honesty

Ⓓ sympathy for others

> Think about what the speaker says in the poem.

Standardized Test Tutor: Reading (Grade 6) © 2009 by Michael Priestley, Scholastic Teaching Resources

Directions: Read this passage about a newspaper story. Then answer questions 19–25.

Don't Believe Everything You Read

WASHINGTON, D.C.—Once, a newspaper writer tried to give Americans a good chuckle. It was 1917, and the United States had just entered World War I. To lift the country's mood of fear and worry, H. L. Mencken invented a history of the bathtub. Henry Louis Mencken was a well-known journalist, editor, and critic of the time. As he said later, he thought people would enjoy his silly story.

Writing for the *New York Evening Mail*, Mencken said that people in this country resisted the tub at first. While many European houses had bathtubs, he wrote, American doctors thought bathing led to sickness. A Cincinnati cotton dealer named Adam Thompson had enjoyed bathing in tubs when he visited England. Thompson became the first American to stand up to doctors and put a bathtub in his own house.

Still the public would not bathe, Mencken declared. In many places, taking a bath was illegal unless a doctor ordered it. The American fear of tubs did not change until 1851. That was the year President Millard Fillmore put a modern bathtub in the White House.

The article set out more details from the bathtub's supposed past, none of them true. No one at the newspaper checked the facts. To his surprise, Mencken's made-up history quickly became accepted as true. Cincinnati began to boast that it was the birthplace of the bathtub. President Fillmore's key role in American plumbing even made it into history books.

Mencken did not reveal the truth until 1926. He said he had never meant for people to believe the story. He thought it was plain to see that the whole thing was a joke. What's more,

Scan the questions before reading so you know what to look for.

Think about the main point of this passage.

he had no idea what the real history of the bathtub was and no interest in finding out. This shamed the editors who printed his story and the writers who repeated it.

Mencken was famous for writing about America's faults. Some people feel that he wrote the story not to amuse people but to show how dumb they could be. If that is true, he proved his point because the story is still fooling people. In October 2003, the *Washington Post* retold the fake bathtub history once again as fact. That was about 80 years after Mencken told the world it wasn't true. A week later, the *Post* issued an apology for any problems this fake story may have caused its readers.

Questions 19–25: Choose the best answer to each question.

19. Which sentence states the main idea of this passage?

    Ⓐ Many American houses have only showers because bathtubs are dangerous.

    Ⓑ America's relationship with the bathtub has had many ups and downs.

    Ⓒ H. L. Mencken wrote a false history of the bathtub that still fools people today.

    Ⓓ H. L. Mencken was a well-known journalist, editor, and critic.

> Think about what you can learn from this passage.

> Compare each sentence to the passage as a whole.

20. According to the passage, which event happened first?

    Ⓐ The *Washington Post* printed the bathtub history without checking the facts first.

    Ⓑ The United States entered World War I.

    Ⓒ Mencken published an article about the history of the bathtub.

    Ⓓ Mencken told the truth about the bathtub story.

> Go back to the passage to find the answer.

21. Which of these resources would be most helpful for researching the history of the bathtub?

    Ⓐ a dictionary   Ⓒ a book of world records

    Ⓑ TV's History Channel   Ⓓ the Internet

> Think about the kinds of information you can find in each source.

Standardized Test Tutor: Reading (Grade 6) © 2009 by Michael Priestley, Scholastic Teaching Resources

22. The passage says, "In many places, taking a bath was *illegal* unless a doctor ordered it." The word *illegal* means—

(A) "against the law."

(B) "not healthful."

(C) "too expensive."

(D) "very enjoyable."

Look at the parts of the word to figure out the answer.

23. According to the passage, H. L. Mencken wrote the history of the bathtub to—

(A) embarrass his readers.

(B) clarify the facts.

(C) make people laugh.

(D) educate the public.

Go back to the beginning of the passage.

24. The title of this passage implies that—

(A) people shouldn't have believed Mencken's article.

(B) the facts in most newspaper articles are wrong.

(C) Internet Web sites are the best places to get the news.

(D) H. L. Mencken caused serious problems with his article.

Think about how the title relates to the events in the passage.

25. Mencken's article about the bathtub is most like which of these?

(A) a published interview of a famous actor

(B) an essay on the need to reduce global warming

(C) an encyclopedia entry about the invention of the telephone

(D) a news story with a fake photo of Bigfoot

Read every answer before you choose one.

Directions: Read this passage about a father and son going to market. Then answer questions 26–32.

A Meeting at Dawn

"A little faster, Tohono," said my father's voice out of the darkness ahead of me. "The first ones on the plaza get the best spots."

I stepped up my pace in response, but a gigantic yawn slowed me down once more. On market days, we started walking in the middle of the night so we could reach Cicuye by morning.

My father, shifting the huge bundle of cloth on his back, passed me a piece of dried meat. I bit into it and started to chew. In the Southwest, dried meat is a staple food for the Tewa people.

The two of us were loaded down with my mother's weaving to trade at the big Cicuye market. Mostly we needed pinto beans, corn, and other foods, but there were many things to see. People from many different Indian tribes came to the market to talk and trade. The Navajos often brought beautiful clay pots or knives made of shiny black obsidian. There might be Apaches trading heaps of buffalo skins. Cicuye, or Pecos Pueblo, as the Spaniards call it, is the biggest pueblo in northern New Spain.

On this day in 1599, we hoped to trade some of our cloth for a metal cooking pot. Spanish soldiers and traders had brought pots, pans, and nails along with their horses and their hunger for land. Often just the presence of a gun-toting soldier on a towering, snorting horse was enough to stop a market-day fight.

When we rounded a bend, the first rays of dawn showed us Cicuye's adobe walls and a small group of travelers ahead. They heard us and stopped. As we approached in the meager light, the shapes revealed themselves as two tall men and a fully loaded mule.

"*Buenos días, amigos!*" said one man. He actually sounded like he did consider us friends. As he bent down to greet us, a large cross swung out on a chain around his neck. He introduced himself as Father Martinez and the other man as Father Guzman.

"*Buenos días,*" said my father, too surprised to say more. What kind of Spaniards were these?

"Bless you! It's wonderful to see people instead of wild pigs!" said Father Guzman, and the two men laughed.

"Oh, did you see many *javelinas*?" my father asked with concern, using the Spanish word for the wild pigs of the desert.

> Look for details that tell about the setting.

> Think about what the characters say and do.

Standardized Test Tutor: Reading (Grade 6) © 2009 by Michael Priestley, Scholastic Teaching Resources

Standardized Test Tutor: Reading (Grade 6) © 2009 by Michael Priestley, Scholastic Teaching Resources

"Yes, quite a few," said Father Martinez. "Very curious animals! They kept us from staying in one place for very long. We haven't slept much since we reached the high desert."

We didn't understand all his words, but his warm, genuine spirit had an effect on us. When we asked how long they had been traveling, Father Martinez said, "Two months over the sea and then hundreds of miles on footpaths. We have been walking for weeks. Thankfully, Niño always finds food for himself."

Niño the mule shifted and brayed, impatient for the end of his long journey. The excitement of Cicuye on market day was no longer the first thing on our minds; the arrival of these strangers changed everything. We walked on with them, drawn by their warmth as they greeted every new face.

So it was that I met Father Martinez and Father Guzman, the first missionaries who came to stay in the land of my ancestors. Their generosity of spirit has brought more Indians to the church door than any number of guns and horses could have. Not all missionaries turned out to be so generous and fair, but I have counted these two men as friends since the day we met.

Questions 26–32: Choose the best answer to each question.

26. What type of passage is this?

Ⓐ folktale

Ⓑ informational article

Ⓒ historical fiction

Ⓓ biography

27. Which detail supports the idea that the Indian tribes are not fighting among themselves?

Ⓐ All of the tribes have common foods, such as dried meat.

Ⓑ Spanish soldiers brought guns and horses to New Spain.

Ⓒ The Navajo, Apache, and Tewa people trade with one another.

Ⓓ The presence of soldiers at the market keeps everything peaceful.

> Does the ending surprise you?

> Think of what you know about each type of literature.

> Read each answer choice to decide which one makes the most sense.

28. Why are Tohono and his father surprised when they meet the priests?

Ⓐ Most Spanish people he has met are soldiers, who do not act friendly.

Ⓑ He doesn't understand the Spanish word *amigos*, meaning "friends."

Ⓒ He isn't used to meeting people on the way to Cicuye.

Ⓓ The local Indians do not behave in such a friendly way.

> Go back to this part of the story.

29. Who is telling this story?

Ⓐ Father Martinez

Ⓑ an outside observer

Ⓒ a Spanish soldier

Ⓓ a grown-up Tewa named Tohono

> Look for clues at the beginning and the end of the story.

30. The passage says, "As we approached in the *meager* light, the shapes revealed themselves as two tall men and a fully loaded mule." In this sentence, the word *meager* suggests that—

Ⓐ the two men look strange.

Ⓑ there is not enough light to see clearly.

Ⓒ the two men have few supplies.

Ⓓ the desert sun is very bright.

> Read the sentences before and after the word to look for clues.

31. The mood of this passage is best described as—

Ⓐ sad.   Ⓒ reflective or thoughtful.

Ⓑ lighthearted.   Ⓓ angry or resentful.

> Think about how the narrator feels at the end.

32. You can infer from the passage that the missionaries are—

Ⓐ good-natured and open to strangers.

Ⓑ worried about their own safety.

Ⓒ starving and thirsty from walking.

Ⓓ determined to take over new lands.

> Check each answer choice against the details in the story.

Directions: Read these two passages about people who work for peace. Then answer questions 33–40.

Passage 1:
Wangari Maathai: Better Living Through Trees

Standardized Test Tutor: Reading (Grade 6) © 2009 by Michael Priestley, Scholastic Teaching Resources

Not many women have won the Nobel Peace Prize. Until 2004, no African woman ever had. That was when Dr. Wangari Maathai won it—for planting trees. You might ask, What do trees have to do with peace?

"Many wars are fought over resources," Dr. Maathai said as she accepted the prize. "If we conserve resources better, the fighting will stop."

Dr. Wangari Maathai started her work in 1977 by planting nine trees in her backyard in Kenya. Trees are important in Africa for several reasons. First, they keep soil from eroding into streams, thus cutting down on pollution, improving the soil, and making shade.

Second, trees provide firewood. So many trees have been cut down in Africa that women must walk far from home to find wood for cooking. New trees can also keep deserts from spreading. Trees help the soil hold water, which makes it easier for small plants to grow. These plants provide food for sheep and cows. Well-fed livestock improve their owners' lives.

Dr. Maathai's Green Belt Movement pays local women for every tree they plant that is still alive three months later. The trees and the money make women's lives better. In its first 15 years, the Green Belt Movement employed at least 50,000 women and planted more than 10 million trees. Following Dr. Maathai's example, the Kenyan government increased its own tree-planting efforts. The movement has spread to 30 countries in Africa, as well as the United States.

When the land and people's lives have improved, Dr. Maathai says, peace will follow.

"Too Hard to Control"

Dr. Maathai was born in Kenya in 1940. Unlike most African women, she went to school. High school woke up a hunger in her for more knowledge. She went to college in Kansas and earned a master's degree in science from the University of Pittsburgh. She became the first Kenyan woman ever to earn a Ph.D., or doctorate of philosophy. Later, Dr. Maathai taught animal science at Kenya's University of Nairobi.

> Skim both passages and the questions before you begin reading.

> Who is Dr. Wangari Maathai and what did she do?

But her life hasn't been all glory. As a young woman, she married a politician and had three children. Her husband divorced her because, he said, she was "too educated, too strong, too successful, too stubborn, and too hard to control." Dr. Maathai has said that African women must not be afraid to show their strength. They must free themselves from silence and fear.

A Responsibility to Lead

Although she began in science, Dr. Maathai's real work has become political. Dr. Maathai has served as a member of parliament in the Kenyan government. Many times she has been beaten and imprisoned, once for stopping a government plan to cut down a forest. However, she believes that it has all been worthwhile.

As an educated woman, Dr. Maathai feels responsible for leading others. She believes that those who understand the environment must act. Our children and grandchildren have a right to a world that is free of pollution and a climate that will support all forms of life.

Passage 2: The Nobel Peace Prize

How does this passage connect to Passage 1?

Alfred Nobel was a successful chemist from Sweden. He invented many kinds of products, including TNT, or dynamite. TNT is a powerful explosive.

Nobel made a lot of money, but he was also a philanthropist. He wanted to help people improve their lives. When he died in 1896, he left millions of dollars in a fund. The money would be used to reward those people each year who benefited humankind most. Prizes would be given for physics, chemistry, medicine, literature, and the promotion of peace.

The first Nobel prizes were awarded in 1901. They have been given out almost every year since then. (A prize in economics was added in 1969.) Each prize is now worth about $1.5 million.

But the Nobel Peace Prize winners have sometimes been controversial. For example, Yasir Arafat shared the prize with two leaders of Israel in 1994. Arafat was a Palestinian who fought against Israel. Many people did not believe that he worked for peace.

Standardized Test Tutor: Reading (Grade 6) © 2009 by Michael Priestley, Scholastic Teaching Resources

The chart below shows some winners of the peace prize.

Recent Winners of the Nobel Peace Prize		
Year	Winner	Nation
2000	Kim Dae Jung	South Korea
2001	United Nations Kofi Annan	United States Ghana
2002	Jimmy Carter	United States
2003	Shirin Ebadi	Iran
2004	Wangari Maathai	Kenya
2005	Mohamed ElBaradei International Atomic Energy Agency	Egypt Austria
2006	Muhammad Yunus Grameen Bank	Bangladesh Bangladesh
2007	Intergovernmental Panel on Climate Change Al Gore	Switzerland United States

Questions 33–40: Choose the best answer to each question.

33. Which sentence states a fact?

    Ⓐ Dr. Wangari Maathai was too successful.

    Ⓑ Dr. Maathai was born in Kenya in 1940.

    Ⓒ Those who understand the environment must act.

    Ⓓ They must free themselves from silence and fear.

> Remember that a fact can be verified.

34. According to Dr. Maathai, how does planting trees lead to peace?

    Ⓐ People are paid to plant trees, so they have plenty of money to spend.

    Ⓑ Trees help to feed cows and sheep, which make their owners feel more peaceful.

    Ⓒ Planting trees improves the soil and holds water, so people have less reason to fight over these resources.

    Ⓓ Planting trees is hard work, so the people who plant and take care of them are too tired to fight.

> Review the passage to find the answer.

Test Tutor says:

35. Which statement would Dr. Wangari Maathai most likely agree with?

    Ⓐ Trees are the most important things on Earth.

    Ⓑ Government leaders usually know what's best for the country.

    Ⓒ Women should work at home and not in the government.

    Ⓓ Human beings must share Earth with all other creatures.

> Find the statement that fits best with what you know about this person.

36. According to Passage 1, how is Dr. Wangari Maathai different from most African women?

    Ⓐ She is well educated.

    Ⓑ She has opinions about government.

    Ⓒ She cares about natural resources.

    Ⓓ She got married and raised a family.

> Skim the passage to find how she is different.

37. The author's main purpose in Passage 1 is to—

    Ⓐ persuade readers to plant trees.

    Ⓑ inform readers about a courageous woman.

    Ⓒ entertain readers with tales of Africa.

    Ⓓ explain the history of the Green Belt Movement.

> Think about why the author wrote this passage.

38. Which Nobel Peace Prize winner was from Egypt?

    Ⓐ Kofi Annan

    Ⓑ Shirin Ebadi

    Ⓒ Mohamed ElBaradei

    Ⓓ Wangari Maathai

> Use the chart to find the answer.

Standardized Test Tutor: Reading (Grade 6) © 2009 by Michael Priestley, Scholastic Teaching Resources

Test Tutor says:

39. Passage 2 says, "But he was also a *philanthropist*." What is a *philanthropist*?

Ⓐ a person who gives money to help others

Ⓑ an organization that awards prizes

Ⓒ a person who works to save the environment

Ⓓ an elected leader of a government

> Look for clues in the sentences before and after the word.

40. Both of these passages focus on which topic?

Ⓐ planting trees

Ⓑ the Green Belt Movement

Ⓒ global warming

Ⓓ the Nobel Peace Prize

> Find the topic that is discussed in both passages, not just one.

End of Test 2 **STOP**

Directions: Read this passage about an unusual well. Then answer questions 1–6.

The Goat Well

There once was a man who was not quite honest. One morning he stopped by a well for a cool drink, but the well was dry. "Bad luck," the scoundrel muttered to himself crossly. Then, adding insult to injury, his only possession—a skinny old goat—slipped and fell into the well.

Before the man could get the creature out of the well, a trader approached. "Please, sir, may I have a cool drink?" asked the newcomer politely.

The quick-witted rogue replied, "Gladly would I share the well, if it were full of water. But this is not an ordinary well. It's a very rare kind of well, a goat well."

Of course the trader had never heard of a goat well. "Surely, you're joking," he protested with a smile.

"You insult my good name, but I speak the truth!" shouted the rogue. "This well, which belongs to my family, is famous. At nightfall, I toss a goat's horn into the well, and at dawn, I pull out a living goat. If you doubt me, come and see for yourself!"

Curious, the trader peered into the well and was amazed to see a goat struggling to climb out of the well. "I see for myself that your strange tale is true," he said, "and I'll not doubt your word again. But tell me, please, how can I acquire such a wonderful well?"

"Didn't I say that it's very rare? There isn't another goat well for a thousand miles. This precious treasure has been passed along from father to son since my great-great-great-grandfather discovered it, and it's not for sale at any price."

Now the cunning scoundrel had planted the idea of a sale, and the trader, as expected, began to bargain for the well. He offered three sacks of grain, then six, and then all the grain he carried. He offered a camel, then three, and then all five that he owned. Finally a deal was struck: all the grain and all the camels in exchange for the rare and valuable well. The trader set up camp, intending to remain by the well, while the dishonest scoundrel prepared to leave, mounted on the finest of the camels.

"Thank you for entrusting me with your family's treasured well, Mr.—what is your name?"

"My name?" asked the rogue. "Call me How-High-I-Can-Leap. That is my name."

Standardized Test Tutor: Reading (Grade 6) © 2009 by Michael Priestley, Scholastic Teaching Resources

Standardized Test Tutor: Reading (Grade 6) © 2009 by Michael Priestley, Scholastic Teaching Resources

At nightfall, the new owner of the well tossed in an old goat's horn. Then he waited impatiently till morning, too excited to sleep. At daybreak there was no goat, so he waited some more; but when noon arrived, he sadly realized he'd been tricked. Without a camel to ride, he walked to the nearest village and inquired of all he met, "Do you know How-High-I-Can-Leap?"

All the villagers replied, "No, show us how high you can leap! Can you leap over this high fence?"

Frustrated, the trader tried to explain what he meant, but each time he repeated his question, the villagers demanded to see him leap. At last he gave up and walked to the next village, and the next, but in every place the same thing happened. Finally, the headman of the farthest village took time to learn the trader's story. It happened that he knew of a man who had five camels and much grain to sell. The village leader sent for this man, telling him to come at once and meet a man called How-Low-I-Shall-Fall.

When the scoundrel arrived, he was taken immediately to the headman. "Why did you summon me?" he asked nervously. "I do not know How-Low-I-Shall-Fall, do you?"

"I certainly do, and soon you will, too," the headman replied. "I order you to return the camels and the grain that you came by dishonestly. Then make a sign saying, 'I am a thief,' hang it around your neck, and walk from village to village. That's how low you shall fall!"

Questions 1–6: Choose the best answer to each question.

1. The passage begins, "There once was a man who was not quite honest." This sentence helps to set a tone, or feeling, of—

   (A) sadness.   (C) anger.

   (B) amusement.   (D) seriousness.

2. The passage says, "Then, adding insult to injury, his only possession—a skinny old goat—slipped and fell into the well." What is the meaning of the phrase *adding insult to injury*?

   (A) mocking or making fun of

   (B) making a bad situation even worse

   (C) causing physical harm

   (D) losing or misplacing something valuable

3. At what point in the story did the scoundrel first realize he might profit from the dry well?

Ⓐ when his great-great-great-grandfather discovered it

Ⓑ as soon as the goat fell into the well

Ⓒ right after the trader began to bargain for the well

Ⓓ when the newcomer asked for a drink

4. Which phrase best describes the trader?

Ⓐ very clever

Ⓑ overly greedy

Ⓒ easily fooled

Ⓓ completely honest

5. The passage says, "Now the cunning scoundrel had *planted* the idea of a sale." Which meaning of the word *plant* best fits in this sentence?

Ⓐ to hide or conceal

Ⓑ to set in the ground to grow

Ⓒ to introduce into one's mind

Ⓓ to place firmly in a position

6. Which sentence best states the theme of the passage?

Ⓐ Cheaters will be punished.

Ⓑ Beware of strangers.

Ⓒ There is no such thing as magic.

Ⓓ It's okay to make mistakes.

Standardized Test Tutor: Reading (Grade 6) © 2009 by Michael Priestley, Scholastic Teaching Resources

Directions: Read this passage about travel. Then answer questions 7–12.

More Travel, Smarter People?

Years ago, famous anthropologist Margaret Mead said, "The traveler who has once been from home is wiser than he who has never left his own doorstep." She believed that people learn from seeing different countries. They benefit and grow from experiencing other cultures.

If this is true, then people must be getting a lot smarter. More people than ever before are visiting other parts of the world. The World Tourism Organization reports that more people travel out of their own country every year. In 2005, there were about 842 million "international arrivals." This is the number of times any traveler comes into a foreign country by air. (A traveler is counted more than once if he flies to a country more than once.) The cost of air travel goes up every year. Yet the airline industry is growing. Profits are up, and so is the total number of passengers.

So where is everyone going, and why? Graph 1 shows that France is the most popular place to go. It had more than 79 million visitors in 2006. Spain is also a very popular destination.

Top 10 Countries Visited in 2006

Some people are surprised to see that the United States is only the third-most-visited country. Still, that adds up to a lot of visitors. In 2006, more than 51 million people came to this country. Some came for vacations. Others came for work or school.

One interesting side note: The United States ranked third in number of visitors but first in total earnings from tourists. This might mean that people who visit the United States stay longer. They may also spend more money than people who visit other countries.

Of course, U.S. citizens are not staying home, either. We also seem to have the travel bug. Americans travel overseas for vacations, for business, and for other reasons. Graph 2 shows the main purposes for U.S. residents' trips abroad in 2006.

Main Purpose of Overseas Trips by U.S. Travelers (2006)

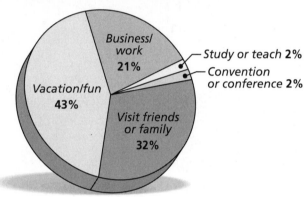

The top two countries that U.S. travelers visit are our neighbors, Mexico and Canada. Of course, many people travel to these countries by car rather than by airplane. Counting only air travelers, more U.S. travelers visit the United Kingdom than any other country.

Questions 7–12: Choose the best answer to each question.

7. According to Margaret Mead, people who travel to other countries tend to—

Ⓐ spend too much money.

Ⓑ learn from their experiences.

Ⓒ enroll in better schools.

Ⓓ earn higher salaries.

8. In this passage, the author is mainly concerned with what kind of travel?

Ⓐ business travel

Ⓒ automobile travel

Ⓑ travel to the United States

Ⓓ international travel

Standardized Test Tutor: Reading (Grade 6) © 2009 by Michael Priestley, Scholastic Teaching Resources

9. According to Graph 1, which of these countries had the *least* number of visitors in 2006?

Ⓐ Russia

Ⓑ Italy

Ⓒ Spain

Ⓓ United Kingdom

10. The most common reason U.S. travelers go to other countries is for—

Ⓐ work.

Ⓑ pleasure.

Ⓒ conferences.

Ⓓ study.

11. The passage says, "Graph 2 shows the main purposes for U.S. residents' trips *abroad* in 2006." What is the meaning of the word *abroad*?

Ⓐ a great distance

Ⓑ several times; repeatedly

Ⓒ to more than one place

Ⓓ out of one's own country

12. Based on this passage, what can you predict about world travel next year?

Ⓐ There will be more travel than this year.

Ⓑ More people will travel by car than by airplane.

Ⓒ The amount of travel will be about the same as this year.

Ⓓ Fewer people will travel to the United States.

Directions: Read this passage about a smelly problem. Then answer questions 13–18.

Joey Solves the Problem

It was still dark, but something pulled Joey out of a deep sleep. "Oh, no," he muttered, "not again!" He jammed a pillow over his head, trying to shut out the awful smell. It didn't work any better than it had last night or the night before. How long will this go on? Joey wondered desperately.

Mom and Dad were awake, too, talking in low voices. None of them had enjoyed a good night's sleep all week.

It was all the fault of their new "neighbor"—a skunk. Last week Joey had seen it creep under the back porch. From there, it must have dug its way under the garage. It was hard to know what happened next. Maybe the skunk made itself at home in another animal's den. Maybe another skunk later found the same warm hideaway. Joey and his family didn't know the reason why the skunk had started to spray directly under their garage. All they knew was that each time it happened, the odor in their house—especially in the rooms nearest the garage—was unbearable. During the day, it was unpleasant. But at night it was far worse. Whoever would have imagined that a *smell* could be powerful enough to wake you from a sound sleep?

In the morning, Mom and Dad talked again. "I hoped the skunk would just leave on its own," Mom said, "but I guess that's not going to happen. We have to do something. If that skunk doesn't move out, I'm going to!"

"I'm coming with you, Mom," said Joey. "How soon can we leave?" Maybe Mom was joking, but Joey wasn't!

Dad opened the telephone book and looked in the yellow pages. "This sounds good: 'Pete's Pest Control: Squirrel, skunk, and bat specialists. Same-day service.' We'll have the problem solved before bedtime. I'll call in the experts. Rescue is on the way!"

Cheered, Joey and Mom left for school and work. They left Dad to talk to the workmen.

But that evening, Dad had bad news. "The pest-control company can trap the skunk and carry it off to the woods. But they won't do that unless they can guarantee their work. And here's the catch: They

Standardized Test Tutor: Reading (Grade 6) © 2009 by Michael Priestley, Scholastic Teaching Resources

can't guarantee their work unless the way back to the den under the garage is closed off. The only way to do that is to install a wire fence around the porch, and it has to extend two feet underground. It means digging up the lawn all around the porch and a price tag of hundreds of dollars. I'm afraid *that* means we'll have to hope the skunk moves out on its own," Dad concluded.

"You mean there's nothing we can do?" asked Mom in disbelief. "What if the skunks *never* leave? What if they raise children and grandchildren and our garage becomes their family home? Someone at work told me skunks can carry rabies. We've got to get rid of them!"

Joey glanced at their old computer and had an idea. Online, he learned that skunks sometimes do carry the dangerous disease rabies. He learned that skunks are good diggers. They dislike bright light, and they like to live under garages and sheds. He browsed a bulletin board where people shared their experiences with skunks. Someone claimed that putting rags soaked in ammonia around a skunk's den would drive it away.

"Let's try this ammonia idea," Joey said, pointing to the screen. "What is ammonia, anyway? Is that the smelly stuff you clean the floor with?"

"Yes," said Dad, "it's powerful stuff. I'll tell you what: you find the rags and put them around the porch. Let me handle the ammonia. Joey, if this works, we'll buy that new computer you've been wishing for!"

They waited till after dark, hoping the skunk was away foraging for food. Then Joey quickly arranged several balled-up rags on the ground around the porch. Dad soaked each one with ammonia. As a final touch, Joey turned on the porch light. "Skunks don't like bright light, so maybe this will help, too," he said.

Tired but hopeful, the family went to bed early.

The next morning, Joey was the first to awaken. He sniffed. There was no odor of skunk. He opened his eyes and saw daylight. "Hooray!" he exclaimed. "It worked!"

Questions 13–18: Choose the best answer to each question.

13. What kind of passage is this?

Ⓐ fantasy   Ⓒ folktale

Ⓑ informational article   Ⓓ realistic fiction

14. Why didn't Dad hire the pest-control company to get rid of the skunk?

    Ⓐ It was going to be too expensive.

    Ⓑ They wouldn't guarantee their work.

    Ⓒ He didn't want to dig up the lawn.

    Ⓓ He thought the skunk would leave on its own.

15. What can you tell about Mom from the dialogue in this passage?

    Ⓐ She would never hurt or trap an animal.

    Ⓑ Using a computer makes her nervous.

    Ⓒ She does not enjoy the job she has.

    Ⓓ The skunk problem really bothers her.

16. What happened after Joey learned about skunks and their habits?

    Ⓐ Dad spoke to the pest-control people.

    Ⓑ Mom went to work and Joey went to school.

    Ⓒ Joey left the porch light on all night.

    Ⓓ The skunk sprayed under the garage again.

17. The passage says, "This sounds good: 'Pete's Pest Control: Squirrel, skunk, and bat *specialists*.'" What is the meaning of the word *specialist*?

    Ⓐ in a distinctive or special manner

    Ⓑ the state of being special

    Ⓒ one with knowledge of a special subject

    Ⓓ not special

18. What will most likely happen next?

    Ⓐ The skunk will return with baby skunks.

    Ⓑ The family will get a new computer.

    Ⓒ Mom will move to another house.

    Ⓓ Joey will try to go back to sleep.

Standardized Test Tutor: Reading (Grade 6) © 2009 by Michael Priestley, Scholastic Teaching Resources

Directions: Read this passage about an American astronaut. Then answer questions 19–25.

Astronaut Visits Hometown

Astronaut Sunita Williams was honored this week in Needham, Massachusetts. That's the town where she grew up. Williams no longer lives in Needham, but her ties to the town remain strong. The 42-year-old astronaut has formed a partnership with a former teacher—and the teacher's lucky students. This year, the teacher's fifth-grade class has followed Williams's career. The students read and listen to news reports about her. They have even exchanged e-mail with her.

On Saturday, the students finally got to see Commander Williams in person. Along with just about everyone in town, they lined the streets for a parade in her honor. In spite of the rain, people smiled and cheered as she passed by and waved.

Clearly, Williams is an inspiring role model. The former navy test pilot flew helicopters in the 1991 Gulf War. Then she became an astronaut with NASA. In December 2006, she boarded the space shuttle *Discovery*. Then she headed to the International Space Station (ISS). Once in space, she broke several records. With 195 days aboard ISS, she has logged the most time in space by a female. Williams also holds the women's record for spacewalking (four walks, totaling 29 hours and 17 minutes).

One day last April, Williams set another record for space travel. Using a special treadmill, she ran 26.2 miles nonstop. That made her the first person ever to run a marathon in space. Yet, in a way, Williams was not running alone. Back on Earth, thousands of people were running, too. They were running a famous race, the Boston Marathon. Williams trained hard for this marathon, both on Earth and in space. Like the runners in Boston, she had an official race number. Hers was 14,000, in honor of her mission, Expedition 14.

Fifth graders in Needham are proud of their hometown heroine, and many are eager to brag about the records she has set. One lesson they have really taken to heart is the importance of exercise and fitness. Taking a cue from Williams's marathon training, the youngsters have been exercising, too. Throughout Williams's time in space, the class set a weekly goal of beating her 11 hours of exercise. In space, exercise is vital to reduce bone and muscle loss. Williams kept fit by running and swimming (through zero gravity instead of water). She also did bike riding and strength training. Working with their gym teacher, the students learned the benefits of exercise on Earth, too. Each student kept an exercise log. They recorded activities such as running, dance, sports, and even walking the family dog.

Most students say it's fun to learn about space. "Someone from my own town is an astronaut," said one youngster. "That's really cool, and it means maybe I could be an astronaut, too!"

Astronaut Sunita Williams has made a lasting impression on these young people, and who knows? Maybe one of them *will* become an astronaut someday.

Questions 19–25: Choose the best answer to each question.

19. The author's main purpose in this passage is to—

   Ⓐ persuade more young students to become astronauts.

   Ⓑ compare Sunita Williams with other astronauts.

   Ⓒ give information about Sunita Williams.

   Ⓓ entertain readers with an exciting story.

20. Which sentence from the passage is an opinion?

   Ⓐ Astronaut Sunita Williams was honored this week in Needham, Massachusetts.

   Ⓑ Clearly, Williams is an inspiring role model.

   Ⓒ With 195 days aboard ISS, she has logged the most time in space by a female.

   Ⓓ Working with their gym teacher, the students learned the benefits of exercise on Earth, too.

Standardized Test Tutor: Reading (Grade 6) © 2009 by Michael Priestley, Scholastic Teaching Resources

21. Which sentence best summarizes the fifth paragraph?

(A) If you are proud of something, it's okay to brag about what you have accomplished.

(B) Students in Needham learned that Sunita Williams was running in a marathon, so they ran in one, too.

(C) Inspired by Sunita Williams, fifth-grade students in Needham are working to increase their fitness.

(D) It is easier to exercise on Earth than in space because gravity helps people become stronger.

22. Which detail from the passage best supports the idea that Williams is willing to help others?

(A) She trained hard in order to do well in the marathon.

(B) She tested aircraft for the U.S. Navy.

(C) She stayed in space longer than any other female.

(D) She exchanged e-mail with young students.

23. The passage says, "One lesson they have really *taken to heart* is the importance of exercise and fitness." What is the meaning of the phrase *take to heart*?

(A) to be strongly affected by something and take it seriously

(B) to do or say something from memory

(C) to cheer up or have more courage or confidence

(D) to be kind, sympathetic, or generous

24. The passage says, "With 195 days aboard ISS, she has *logged* the most time in space by a female." Which dictionary definition of *log* best fits this sentence?

> **log** *noun* **1.** a portion or length of a tree trunk. **2.** a record of details for a trip by airplane or ship. *verb* **3.** to cut down trees or timber. **4.** to travel for a certain distance or time.

(A) definition 1

(B) definition 2

(C) definition 3

(D) definition 4

25. To learn more about Sunita Williams's work aboard the ISS, which would be the best place to look?

(A) an encyclopedia

(B) the NASA Web site

(C) *The World Almanac*

(D) a thesaurus

Standardized Test Tutor: Reading (Grade 6) © 2009 by Michael Priestley, Scholastic Teaching Resources

Directions: Read this passage about a king's judgment. Then answer questions 26–32.

Fair Payment

Long ago, a king decided that a grand bazaar should take place on the grounds of his royal palace. On the appointed day, merchants and craftspeople set out their wares in the palace yard. Strolling musicians played lively tunes as jugglers and magicians performed their acts. Cooks prepared food over open fires, and the aroma of their offerings drifted through the air.

The king's subjects came from far and wide to enjoy the bazaar. One of them was a young peasant named Luke. Two days had passed since Luke had last eaten, and he was terribly hungry. A softhearted baker who was selling bread at the bazaar saw Luke and took pity on him. He cut a thick slice of molasses bread and offered it to the hungry man.

Luke brought the slice to his mouth and was about to gobble it down when he suddenly changed his mind. He walked through the crowded bazaar, sniffing the air and looking this way and that until he spotted a cook who was tending a steaming kettle of lamb stew. Luke made his way over to the kettle and held his slice of bread above it for several minutes, letting it absorb the flavor of the rising steam. When Luke finally ate the slice, he sighed with satisfaction.

The cook, however, was furious. He stretched an open palm in front of Luke's nose and jabbed at it with his other hand. "You must pay me for what you took from my kettle!" he demanded.

"I took nothing but the steam," Luke insisted. "You may as well ask me to pay for the air I breathe."

Luke and the cook argued back and forth, their voices growing steadily louder. Soon a crowd assembled around them. As they listened to the dispute, some in the crowd took the cook's side, but the rest favored Luke.

Finally, the cook grabbed Luke by the elbow and steered him toward the king's palace. "Our king is famous for his wisdom and fairness," he said, "so we shall present our case to him and let him determine which of us is right."

Before long, Luke and the cook were standing before the king. As each man gave his version of the events, the king listened attentively. Then he sat silently for several moments as he reflected on what he had heard.

Finally, the king looked at both men and declared, "It is my judgment that something has indeed been taken from the cook, and so he should be paid for it."

Hearing these words, the cook made a deep bow to the king and then smiled smugly at Luke. But the king had not finished speaking.

"Of course," he continued, "that payment should equal the value of what the hungry man has taken from the cook." With that, the king reached into his robe, pulled out two coins, and showed them to the men. Closing his fingers around the coins, the king shook them so they jingled.

Then the king looked at the cook and said, "If two coins are fair payment for a serving of stew, then the jingle of two coins is fair payment for the steam from the stew. So, you have now received fair payment for what was taken from you."

Questions 26–32: Choose the best answer to each question.

26. Which detail is a clue that this passage is a folktale?

   Ⓐ The story begins with the phrase "Long ago."

   Ⓑ Two characters have a disagreement.

   Ⓒ All of the events take place in one day.

   Ⓓ The characters in the story speak.

27. The passage says, "Cooks prepared food over open fires, and the *aroma* of their offerings drifted through the air." In this sentence, the word *aroma* suggests a smell that is—

   Ⓐ rotten.

   Ⓑ unusual.

   Ⓒ alarming.

   Ⓓ pleasing.

28. Luke held the bread over the steaming kettle to—

   Ⓐ change its color.

   Ⓑ clean it.

   Ⓒ make it more flavorful.

   Ⓓ bake it.

Standardized Test Tutor: Reading (Grade 6) © 2009 by Michael Priestley, Scholastic Teaching Resources

29. Which character demonstrates kindness and generosity?

Ⓐ the baker

Ⓑ Luke

Ⓒ the cook

Ⓓ the king

30. The cook's complaint in this story is most like which of these family situations?

Ⓐ A brother gets upset when his sister plays with a toy he isn't using.

Ⓑ A brother and sister argue about which television program to watch.

Ⓒ A sister gets upset when her brother borrows her watch and loses it.

Ⓓ A brother and sister argue about who gets to eat the last slice of pie.

31. How did the cook probably feel when the king decided that the jingle of two coins was fair payment for the steam from his stew?

Ⓐ timid and afraid

Ⓑ amused and relieved

Ⓒ shocked and disappointed

Ⓓ happy and grateful

32. What lesson does this story teach?

Ⓐ Keep your opinions to yourself.

Ⓑ Wise people have much success in life.

Ⓒ Thieves are all around us.

Ⓓ Don't make a big fuss about a small matter.

Directions: Read these two passages about the ship *Titanic*.
Then answer questions 33–40.

Passage 1: Titanic Troubles

The luxury ship *Titanic* sank off the coast of Newfoundland in
1912. It is the world's most famous shipwreck. The *Titanic's* builders
had bragged that it could not sink, yet the ship went down on its first
voyage. Due to a shortage of lifeboats, more than 1,500 passengers
perished with the *Titanic*. Many of the 705 surviving passengers told
poignant stories of leaving loved ones behind on the sinking ship.

For 73 years, the *Titanic* rested undisturbed at the bottom of the
Atlantic Ocean. Many adventurers dreamed of finding the ship, but
no one knew exactly where it was. Some said the *Titanic* could never
be found. Others were more hopeful, but they knew that finding
the *Titanic* would take more than luck. It would take highly trained
scientists and state-of-the-art equipment.

In 1981, oceanographer Robert Ballard made up his mind to
find the *Titanic*. He started by putting together a team of scientists.
Then Ballard and his team set about building *Argo-Jason*. This robot
submarine was a bit larger than a car. It had video cameras and
operated by remote control.

By August 1985, the team was ready. They launched *Argo-Jason*
from a ship in the North Atlantic in the area where the *Titanic* sank.
Just a few days later, the submarine's cameras sent up pictures of the
wrecked ship on the ocean floor. Along with the rusted ship itself, the
pictures showed items such as dishes, silverware, and shoes.

The *Titanic's* discovery thrilled the whole world. Over the years,
it has drawn many tourists who come to see the wreck up close.
Some pay thousands of dollars to view the *Titanic* from a submarine.

Standardized Test Tutor: Reading (Grade 6) © 2009 by Michael Priestley, Scholastic Teaching Resources

Others put on diving gear and swim around the ship. Sadly, tourism has been bad for the *Titanic*. Parts of the ship have been stolen or damaged. The ocean floor is littered with plastic flowers and other items left there by tourists.

What can be done to protect the *Titanic*? Some people want tourists to follow a "look but don't touch" policy at the site. Others say tourists should not be allowed to visit the site anymore. However, solutions like these are hard to carry out at the bottom of the ocean. At this point, damage to the *Titanic* is likely to continue.

Passage 2: Undersea Explorer

Robert Ballard was born in 1942. From an early age, he loved the sea. Ballard grew up in Southern California. He spent his free time at the beach near his home. He enjoyed fishing and swimming. He even learned to scuba dive.

When Ballard wasn't at the ocean, he loved reading about it. At age 10, he read *20,000 Leagues Under the Sea*. That was one of the first science-fiction books. It describes the undersea adventures of Captain Nemo. Nemo was a scientist and the captain of a submarine disguised as a whale.

Ballard decided he wanted to be like Captain Nemo when he grew up. His parents helped him follow his dream. They encouraged him to become an oceanographer. That is a person who studies the oceans.

Ballard was a hardworking student. He spent many years learning all he could about the ocean. By the age of 28, he was an expert. In 1970, he took a job as a scientist at Woods Hole Oceanographic Institute in Massachusetts. There he studied underwater mountains of the Atlantic Ocean. He came up with ways to predict volcanoes under the oceans. Working with other scientists, Ballard also found previously unknown sea animals. These animals lived far below the ocean's surface, where scientists had believed no animals could live.

By the 1980s, Ballard's interests changed. He developed unmanned vehicles to explore the ocean's depths. His first find, the luxury ship *Titanic*, made Ballard famous. He was not happy with just one big find, however. He looked for—and found—other well-known ships. One was the German battleship *Bismarck*. Another was the *U.S.S. Yorktown*, an aircraft carrier that sank during World War II.

Standardized Test Tutor: Reading (Grade 6) © 2009 by Michael Priestley, Scholastic Teaching Resources

Today Robert Ballard is still an underwater explorer. He also heads an organization that encourages students to learn about science. Ballard hopes that some of the students will follow in his footsteps. After all, the world's huge oceans are mostly unexplored. Who knows what remains to be discovered under the sea?

Questions 33–40: Choose the best answer to each question.

33. Passage 1 says, "Many of the 705 surviving passengers told *poignant* stories of leaving loved ones behind on the sinking ship." What does *poignant* mean?

   Ⓐ believable   Ⓒ interesting

   Ⓑ emotional   Ⓓ resentful

34. Which detail from Passage 1 shows the difficulty of finding the *Titanic*?

   Ⓐ It is the world's most famous shipwreck.

   Ⓑ More than 1,500 passengers perished with the *Titanic*.

   Ⓒ It would take highly trained scientists and state-of-the-art equipment.

   Ⓓ In 1981, oceanographer Robert Ballard made up his mind to find the *Titanic*.

35. Which sentence best describes what the author of Passage 1 thinks about tourists who visit the *Titanic* site?

   Ⓐ They are wasting their money.

   Ⓑ They should treat the site with more respect.

   Ⓒ They are sure to have a wonderful time.

   Ⓓ They are brave and adventurous explorers.

36. The information in Passage 1 is mostly organized by—

   Ⓐ comparison and contrast.   Ⓒ chronological order.

   Ⓑ classification.   Ⓓ cause and effect.

37. Which reference source should you use to find out where the *Titanic* sailed from and where it was heading when it sank?

   Ⓐ an encyclopedia   Ⓒ an atlas

   Ⓑ a dictionary   Ⓓ a thesaurus

Standardized Test Tutor: Reading (Grade 6) © 2009 by Michael Priestley, Scholastic Teaching Resources

38. Which is the best summary of Passage 2?

  Ⓐ Robert Ballard loved to swim and fish as a child. Then he read about Captain Nemo and decided to become an oceanographer.

  Ⓑ Robert Ballard read *20,000 Leagues Under the Sea* and decided to become an oceanographer. His parents helped him follow his dream. Then Ballard found the *Titanic*.

  Ⓒ Robert Ballard is a real-life Captain Nemo. He knows a lot about the ocean, and he wants young people to learn about science.

  Ⓓ Robert Ballard loved the ocean and became an oceanographer. He studied underwater volcanoes and sea animals, but he is most famous for finding the *Titanic* and other ships.

39. What did Ballard do just before he found the *Titanic*?

  Ⓐ He studied underwater mountains of the Atlantic Ocean.

  Ⓑ He discovered sea animals far beneath the ocean's surface.

  Ⓒ He developed unmanned vehicles to explore the ocean's depths.

  Ⓓ He found ways to predict volcanoes under the ocean.

40. Which sentence states an important focus in both of these passages?

  Ⓐ The *Titanic* was supposed to be unsinkable, but it sank on its first voyage.

  Ⓑ Robert Ballard has made some great discoveries in the world's oceans.

  Ⓒ The *Titanic*, the *Bismarck*, and the *U.S.S. Yorktown* were all famous ships.

  Ⓓ Robert Ballard took pictures of the *Titanic* on the bottom of the ocean.

End of Test 3   **STOP**

Standardized Test Tutor: Reading

Answer Sheet

Grade **6**

Student Name _____

Teacher Name _____

Test 1 2 3

(circle one)

Directions: Fill in the bubble for the answer you choose.

1. Ⓐ Ⓑ Ⓒ Ⓓ   15. Ⓐ Ⓑ Ⓒ Ⓓ   29. Ⓐ Ⓑ Ⓒ Ⓓ

2. Ⓐ Ⓑ Ⓒ Ⓓ   16. Ⓐ Ⓑ Ⓒ Ⓓ   30. Ⓐ Ⓑ Ⓒ Ⓓ

3. Ⓐ Ⓑ Ⓒ Ⓓ   17. Ⓐ Ⓑ Ⓒ Ⓓ   31. Ⓐ Ⓑ Ⓒ Ⓓ

4. Ⓐ Ⓑ Ⓒ Ⓓ   18. Ⓐ Ⓑ Ⓒ Ⓓ   32. Ⓐ Ⓑ Ⓒ Ⓓ

5. Ⓐ Ⓑ Ⓒ Ⓓ   19. Ⓐ Ⓑ Ⓒ Ⓓ   33. Ⓐ Ⓑ Ⓒ Ⓓ

6. Ⓐ Ⓑ Ⓒ Ⓓ   20. Ⓐ Ⓑ Ⓒ Ⓓ   34. Ⓐ Ⓑ Ⓒ Ⓓ

7. Ⓐ Ⓑ Ⓒ Ⓓ   21. Ⓐ Ⓑ Ⓒ Ⓓ   35. Ⓐ Ⓑ Ⓒ Ⓓ

8. Ⓐ Ⓑ Ⓒ Ⓓ   22. Ⓐ Ⓑ Ⓒ Ⓓ   36. Ⓐ Ⓑ Ⓒ Ⓓ

9. Ⓐ Ⓑ Ⓒ Ⓓ   23. Ⓐ Ⓑ Ⓒ Ⓓ   37. Ⓐ Ⓑ Ⓒ Ⓓ

10. Ⓐ Ⓑ Ⓒ Ⓓ   24. Ⓐ Ⓑ Ⓒ Ⓓ   38. Ⓐ Ⓑ Ⓒ Ⓓ

11. Ⓐ Ⓑ Ⓒ Ⓓ   25. Ⓐ Ⓑ Ⓒ Ⓓ   39. Ⓐ Ⓑ Ⓒ Ⓓ

12. Ⓐ Ⓑ Ⓒ Ⓓ   26. Ⓐ Ⓑ Ⓒ Ⓓ   40. Ⓐ Ⓑ Ⓒ Ⓓ

13. Ⓐ Ⓑ Ⓒ Ⓓ   27. Ⓐ Ⓑ Ⓒ Ⓓ

14. Ⓐ Ⓑ Ⓒ Ⓓ   28. Ⓐ Ⓑ Ⓒ Ⓓ

Standardized Test Tutor: Reading (Grade 6). © 2009 by Michael Priestley, Scholastic Teaching Resources

Test 1 Answer Key

1. C	**11.** C	**21.** C	**31.** A
2. B	**12.** D	**22.** C	**32.** B
3. D	**13.** B	**23.** B	**33.** D
4. A	**14.** B	**24.** A	**34.** C
5. A	**15.** D	**25.** B	**35.** C
6. B	**16.** C	**26.** C	**36.** B
7. D	**17.** A	**27.** A	**37.** A
8. A	**18.** C	**28.** C	**38.** D
9. B	**19.** D	**29.** B	**39.** D
10. A	**20.** A	**30.** D	**40.** A

Answer Key Explanations

A Tough Decision

1. Correct response: **C**
(*Analyze literary elements: plot*)
The narrator wonders whether she made the right decision, and the title refers to this same conflict.

Incorrect choices:

A The narrator wonders if she cheated, but no one accuses her of doing so.

B This is a smaller problem that is resolved with a playoff.

D The story says that "everybody" agreed this was a fair way to decide.

2. Correct response: **B**
(*Identify cause and effect*)
Too many students showed up for the meeting, so Mr. Gaudi decided they would need a playoff to choose the team.

Incorrect choices:

A The students answered practice questions to choose the team, not to prepare for the game show.

C The narrator and Carla signed up before the meeting, not as a result of it.

D The *Smart Aleck* show required five team members; Mr. Gaudi did not decide on this number as a result of the meeting.

3. Correct response: **D**
(*Compare and contrast*)
　　Both girls are smart and are well qualified for the team.

Incorrect choices:

A The passage says that both girls record *Smart Aleck* and watch it when they get home, but it does not say they go straight home after school.

B The passage says that Carla is imaginative, but not the narrator.

C The narrator makes a sacrifice for Carla, but Carla does not make a sacrifice.

4. Correct response: **A**
(*Use prefixes and suffixes to determine word meaning*)
　　The suffix -*or* is a noun suffix that refers to a person.

Incorrect choices:

B A word meaning "not competing" would have a negative prefix, such as *un*-.

C The -*or* suffix does not refer to a place.

D A word meaning "before competing" would begin with the prefix *pre*- or *ante*-.

5. Correct response: **A**
(*Identify sequence of events*)
　　The students met in Mr. Gaudi's office and learned that there were too many students. Next, they competed in a playoff.

Incorrect choices:

B Students met in Mr. Gaudi's office before they learned there were too many students.

C The school was selected to compete before anyone signed up.

D Carla and the narrator signed up as soon as they heard that the school had been selected, a few days before the meeting in Mr. Gaudi's office.

6. Correct response: **B**
(*Analyze literary elements: narrative point of view*)
　　In this sentence, the narrator refers to herself ("I") and the decision she made, so this would not be included in a passage told from Carla's point of view.

Incorrect choices:

A Either Carla or the narrator could say this about themselves ("we").

C and **D** could have been made by either Carla or the narrator.

Where Have All the Chestnuts Gone?

7. Correct response: **D**
(*Identify main idea and details*)
　　The main idea of this article is stated in the first paragraph.

Incorrect choices:

A This sentence gives a detail from the last paragraph of the passage.

B This is a detail sentence, not the main idea.

C This is a supporting detail but not the main idea.

8. Correct response: **A**
(*Interpret graphic features: diagrams*)
　　These pictures show a chestnut tree before and after the blight.

Incorrect choices:

B It could describe the first illustration but not the second.

C The second picture shows the result of the blight but does not explain it.

D This could describe the second picture but not the first.

9. Correct response: **B**

(*Make inferences, predictions, or generalizations*)

The third paragraph explains that entire communities depended on the chestnut for income, and they likely suffered hardships when the chestnuts started to die.

Incorrect choices:

A Native Americans may have stopped using chestnut trees, but the passage does not suggest that they stopped using all kinds of tree bark and leaves.

C The passage says that the blight affected only the American chestnut.

D Scientists now encourage people to plant American chestnuts, but the passage provides no information about how many were planted in earlier years.

10. Correct response: **A**

(*Distinguish fact and opinion*)

This sentence states a personal view ("tastiness") that cannot be verified as fact.

Incorrect choices:

B, **C**, and **D** state facts about the American chestnut that can be proven true.

11. Correct response: **C**

(*Use details or evidence from the text to support ideas*)

Squirrels are small animals that can't jump long distances, so the trees must have been close together.

Incorrect choices:

A The number of acres does not tell how close the trees were.

B Trees that grow this large are not likely to be too close together.

D Each tree provided good shade by itself, so this does not mean that the trees grew close together.

12. Correct response: **D**

(*Identify text structure/organization*)

The information is organized mainly in time sequence, from before 1900 to the early 1900s to today.

Incorrect choices:

A The pictures make a comparison, but the information in the text is not organized this way.

B The article says that the blight came to the United States from Asia, but this is a factual detail and not the organizational structure for the article.

C The article mentions some causes and effects in the fourth and fifth paragraphs, but the article as a whole is not organized this way.

At the Aquarium and In March

13. Correct response: **B**

(*Analyze literary elements: narrative point of view*)

In lines 1–6, the speaker describes the fish from his point of view. Beginning in line 7, the fish ("They") are watching the people "in the air" (above the water).

Incorrect choices:

A, **C**, and **D** are other things that people could be looking at, but the point of view changes from the people's perspective to the fishes' perspective.

14. Correct response: **B**

(*Evaluate author's point of view*)

The fish swim "to and fro" and "have no pathway where they go." The people "wander also to and fro, / And know not why or where they go."

14. (continued)
Incorrect choices:

A This statement may be true, but the speaker does not suggest this idea in the poem.

C The poem actually hints that neither the people nor the fish are suited to their environments because they wander back and forth and don't know where to go.

D The speaker observes both fish and people at an aquarium, but the poem does not suggest that he found one more interesting than the other.

15. Correct response: **D**
(*Identify the use of literary devices*)
The poem refers to "ripples" stirred by the music and the shallow breaking of waves.

Incorrect choices:

A The poem says that warm days are near, but it does not compare the song to warm days.

B The poem describes the bird as "blue-backed" but does not compare the song to color.

C The poem does not compare the bird and its song to each other.

16. Correct response: **C**
(*Analyze literary elements: plot*)
The setting of the poem is March, and "Warm days are near!" means spring is coming.

Incorrect choices:

A The poem mentions a fence-post, but this is not the topic of the poem.

B The poem describes the sound of birdsong, but this is not the main topic.

D The speaker feels warmth or joy when listening to the bird, not a broken heart.

17. Correct response: **A**
(*Interpret poetry and its characteristics*)
This line uses alliteration by repeating the "s" sound in *serene* and *silver*.

Incorrect choices:

B, **C**, and **D** do not use alliteration.

18. Correct response: **C**
(*Make connections*)
Both poems use the same rhyme scheme (*aabbcc . . .*).

Incorrect choices:

A The first poem describes fish in an aquarium, and the second poem describes a bird on a fence-post.

B The mood in the first poem is quiet and somewhat disturbing, while the mood in the second poem is warm and pleasant.

D The second poem is an example of free verse (it does not have a regular metrical pattern), but the first poem is not.

A Story of Hope

19. Correct response: **D**
(*Identify main idea and details*)
The passage focuses on the enduring popularity of Ebenezer Scrooge as a film and stage character.

Incorrect choices:

A This sentence is a detail from the first paragraph, not the main idea.

B This sentence is a detail from the second paragraph, not the main idea.

C This sentence gives a supporting detail but not the main idea.

20. Correct response: **A**
(*Distinguish essential and nonessential information*)

This detail is not essential because the rest of the passage talks about how popular the story is and has been since 1843.

Incorrect choices:

B Knowing when the story was written helps readers appreciate how long it has been popular.

C This detail helps the reader understand that the story of *A Christmas Carol* was adapted to other media from the beginning and quite often after that.

D This detail emphasizes the continuing popularity of the story.

21. Correct response: **C**
(*Distinguish denotative and connotative meanings*)

The word *dashed* clearly suggests that something was done in a hurry or in a short time.

Incorrect choices:

A The book had not yet been written so it could not be destroyed.

B "Ran or sprinted" is one meaning of *dashed*, but it does not fit the context of this sentence.

D The phrase *dashed off* refers to the manner in which the story was written, not the handwriting.

22. Correct response: **C**
(*Identify sequence of events*)

As described in paragraph 5, Scrooge became generous and caring after his experience with the three spirits.

Incorrect choices:

A The second spirit takes him to his nephew's home.

B The second spirit also showed him the poor people of London.

D He received a warning from Marley before his experiences with the spirits.

23. Correct response: **B**
(*Use details or evidence from the text to support ideas*)

For a book to sell out so quickly (especially in the nineteenth century), people must have already known and liked the author's works.

Incorrect choices:

A He did not stage the play until the year after he wrote the book.

C He could be an "English author" without being popular.

D This detail only shows that *A Christmas Carol* is still popular.

24. Correct response: **A**
(*Use context clues to determine word meaning*)

The examples of actors given in the sixth paragraph make the meaning clear.

Incorrect choices:

B, **C**, and **D** could fit into the sentence grammatically, but they do not fit the meaning.

25. Correct response: **B**
(*Summarize*)

This is the best summary of the entire passage.

Incorrect choices:

A These sentences do not mention Scrooge or his popularity in movies and on stage.

C These sentences focus only on the writing and sale of *A Christmas Carol*.

D These sentences do not mention the author, Scrooge, or the plot of the story.

The Silver Mouse

26. Correct response: **C**
(*Identify literary genres and their characteristics*)
The story begins with "Once upon a time," involves the use of magic, includes a talking mouse, and ends with a moral lesson learned. These are all characteristics of a folktale.

Incorrect choices:

A An essay is nonfiction and does not include characters or a plot.

B Science fiction involves technology and is usually set in the future.

D A biography tells the life story of a real person.

27. Correct response: **A**
(*Identify cause and effect*)
He let the mouse go because of its "anxious look," which suggests that he felt sorry for it.

Incorrect choices:

B The mouse never bit Gregory or even tried to escape.

C Gregory was on his way to the playground, but he did not seem to be in a hurry.

D Gregory let the mouse go before the mouse granted his wish.

28. Correct response: **C**
(*Interpret figurative language, including idioms*)
Having someone "under your thumb" is an idiom meaning "dominating or having complete control of."

Incorrect choices:

A, **B**, and **D** are literal interpretations related to a person's thumb, but they do not fit the meaning of the idiom.

29. Correct response: **B**
(*Analyze characters*)
As described in the sixth paragraph, Gregory was reluctant because he thought his mother was asking for too much.

29. (continued)
Incorrect choices:

A Gregory does not think of or mention his friends when he goes to talk to the mouse, so he is not afraid that they will see him.

C The mouse always gave him what he asked for, so Gregory had no reason to think that the mouse would not respond.

D Gregory did not really want to live in the suburbs, but this was not why he felt reluctant; he felt reluctant every time, not just when he asked for a new house.

30. Correct response: **D**
(*Analyze characters*)
The mouse's comments change from friendly ("Did you like the TV?") to mildly sarcastic ("Let me guess") to irritated ("What now?").

Incorrect choices:

A The mouse grants each wish and does not argue about it.

B The mouse always arrives immediately when Gregory calls.

C There are no descriptions of how the mouse's face looked.

31. Correct response: **A**
(*Analyze literary elements: setting*)
Of the four choices, the high-definition television is the only one unique to modern times.

Incorrect choices:

B A silver mouse gives no indication of when the story takes place.

C A playground suggests a setting in the last 100 years or so, but it would not have to be very recent.

D Boxes and suitcases suggest a setting in the last 200 years or so, but not as recent as an HDTV.

32. Correct response: **B**
(*Analyze literary elements: theme*)
   The theme can be inferred from the mouse's last statement: "You could have had anything within reason. But instead, your greediness has returned you to where you started."

Incorrect choices:

A This is a popular proverb but does not relate to this story.

C This story involves a sense of "home," but this is not the theme.

D This theme does not relate to the message of this story.

So You Want to Donate Blood and Student Council Holds Blood Drive

33. Correct response: **D**
(*Use prefixes and suffixes to determine word meaning*)
   People who need blood get a *transfusion*, or a transfer of blood from one person to another.

Incorrect choices:

A, **B**, and **C** are incorrect. Patients may need all of these things, but they do not fit the meaning of *transfusion*.

34. Correct response: **C**
(*Use text features*)
   This section tells what is done with donated blood and how it is stored.

Incorrect choices:

A This section tells why people need blood, not how it is stored.

B This section tells how blood is drawn.

D This section tells how young people can help with blood donation.

35. Correct response: **C**
(*Identify cause and effect*)
   The fifth paragraph explains that tightening the strap makes a person's veins stick out.

Incorrect choices:

A Loosening the band, not tightening it, causes the blood to flow freely.

B Feeling light-headed is an effect of giving blood, not of tightening the strap.

D The donor squeezes the rubber ball to help the veins stick out, but being able to squeeze the ball is not caused by tightening the strap.

36. Correct response: **B**
(*Evaluate author's purpose*)
   As the title indicates, this passage is a flyer or poster written to encourage students to help with the blood drive.

Incorrect choices:

A The passage says that donors must be healthy, but it was not written to help students stay healthy.

C This passage is not a story written to entertain.

D Passage 1 gives information about donating blood, but this passage tells how students can help.

37. Correct response: **A**
(*Make connections*)
   A student trying to recruit donors for a blood drive would benefit most from the information given in Passage 1, which he or she could use to answer a potential donor's questions.

Incorrect choices:

B This is a small detail in the passage but not its most helpful feature.

C Planning entertainment is mentioned in Passage 2 but not in Passage 1.

D The passage mentions three kinds of snacks, but this is not its most helpful feature.

38. Correct response: **D**
(*Use context clues to determine meaning of multiple-meaning words*)
   Passage 2 describes things that students can do to help with a blood drive, so "a scheduled period of work" best fits the meaning of *shift* in this context.

Incorrect choices:

A, **B**, and **C** are other definitions of the word *shift*, but none fits the context of this sentence.

39. Correct response: **D**
(*Make inferences*)
   Based on the information in Passage 1, you can infer that they need 65 people because some of the people may not be qualified to give blood.

Incorrect choices:

A Some of the donors may not feel well after giving blood, but this would not require having extra people to obtain 50 pints.

B This is probably true, but people who do not like the idea would not come in to donate anyway.

C Blood is handled very carefully and is not likely to be lost or spilled.

40. Correct response: **A**
(*Compare and contrast*)
   Both passages describe ways that young people can help.

Incorrect choices:

B The information in Passage 2 is written specifically for students, but one can't really say which passage is more useful to all students.

C Passage 1 gives detailed information about the process, but Passage 2 does not.

D Passage 1 encourages people to give blood, but Passage 2 focuses on trying to get young people (who are probably too young to donate blood) to help with a blood drive.

Test ② Answer Key

1. B	**11.** C	**21.** D	**31.** C
2. C	**12.** A	**22.** A	**32.** A
3. B	**13.** C	**23.** C	**33.** B
4. A	**14.** B	**24.** A	**34.** C
5. D	**15.** B	**25.** D	**35.** D
6. A	**16.** D	**26.** C	**36.** A
7. D	**17.** A	**27.** C	**37.** B
8. D	**18.** D	**28.** A	**38.** C
9. C	**19.** C	**29.** D	**39.** A
10. B	**20.** B	**30.** B	**40.** D

Answer Key Explanations

The Bridge of the Gods

1. Correct response: **B**
(*Identify cause and effect*)
The Great Spirit became angry when the tribes fought over who would marry Lewit.

Incorrect choices:

A The Great Spirit answered the chiefs' prayers with new land for both tribes.

C The story does not say the tribes thanked the Great Spirit, but it also doesn't mention that this was a problem.

D The tribes used the bridge often and seemed to be happy about it.

2. Correct response: **C**
(*Identify sequence of events*)
After the Great Spirit grants their prayers, the chiefs shoot arrows to claim their new land.

Incorrect choices:

A Lewit shares her fire years after the Great Spirit builds the bridge.

B Klickitat brings a gift to Lewit after she shares her fire.

D The Great Spirit builds the bridge after the chiefs shoot their arrows.

3. Correct response: **B**
(*Analyze characters*)
The Great Spirit is fair because he does not favor one tribe over the other. His kindness shows when he gives the tribes new lands, the Bridge of the Gods, and fire.

3. (continued)
Incorrect choices:

A The Great Spirit shows no signs of being greedy.

C The Great Spirit takes care of the people, so he is not cold and distant.

D The Great Spirit acts fairly toward the people, so he is not unjust or cruel.

4. Correct response: **A**
(*Make inferences*)

At the beginning, Lewit was the only one who had fire and she lived by herself, so neither tribe could have cooked their food.

Incorrect choices:

B The two chiefs prayed together, so they must have gotten along.

C At the beginning, the tribes had "fallen on hard times," so their lives were not happy and peaceful.

D The two tribes traded together for years after the bridge was built, so they probably had things to trade earlier.

5. Correct response: **D**
(*Use reference aids to clarify meaning: dictionary*)

The passage says that the tribes hunted and fished in the Columbia River area and food was plentiful, so the word *game* must refer to animals that are hunted.

Incorrect choices:

A, **B**, and **C** are all definitions of the word *game*, but they do not fit the context of this sentence.

6. Correct response: **A**
(*Analyze literary elements: theme*)

The people become unhappy when they fight over something they do not or cannot have (Lewit).

6. (continued)
Incorrect choices:

B Lewit as a young woman may not be what she seems, but this is not the main point of the story.

C This saying about the power of faith does not apply to this story.

D This story is not about patience or waiting, and the main characters do not get what they want in the end.

Wondrous, Dangerous Plastic

7. Correct response: **D**
(*Summarize*)

This sentence is the best summary of the paragraph.

Incorrect choices:

A and **B** are details from the paragraph, but they both omit the point that no one knows how long plastic will take to break down.

C This example was mentioned in the paragraph as an "if," but there was no plastic in Washington's day.

8. Correct response: **D**
(*Evaluate author's purpose*)

The author wants readers to think about how plastic affects the world and reduce their use of plastic.

Incorrect choices:

A The passage names the main ingredient in plastic but does not explain how it is made.

B The author doesn't fault the makers or users of plastic.

C The author does compare plastic with other products in the third and fourth paragraphs, but this is not the main purpose of the passage.

9. Correct response: **C**
(*Distinguish denotative and connotative meanings*)
The word *flimsy* suggests that these bags are made poorly and cheaply because they are used once and thrown away.

Incorrect choices:

A The sentence contradicts this meaning because the bags are used only once.

B The word *precious* indicates that oil is very valuable.

D Oil may be hard to find but shopping bags are not.

10. Correct response: **B**
(*Recognize bias, persuasion, and propaganda*)
This rhetorical question clearly reveals the author's feeling that animals are more important than the convenience of plastic products.

Incorrect choices:

A This statement could be viewed as the author's opinion, but it does not reveal the author's bias as clearly as choice B.

C and **D** are factual statements that do not reveal the author's viewpoint or bias.

11. Correct response: **C**
(*Interpret graphic features: chart*)
Cutting plastic into pieces is not included in the chart as a way to reduce plastic in the environment, and it could be harmful to birds, animals, and fish that might eat the plastic.

Incorrect choices:

A, **B**, and **D** are all listed in the chart as good ways to reduce the amount of plastic in the environment.

12. Correct response: **A**
(*Use details or evidence from the text to support ideas*)
This detail gives a clear example of how plastic can be dangerous.

Incorrect choices:

B The fact that plastic is useful does not make it dangerous.

C This fact supports the idea that plastic is widely used, but that does not make it dangerous.

D This detail tells who made the first plastic and does not suggest that it is dangerous.

The House With Nobody in It

13. Correct response: **C**
(*Analyze literary elements: plot*)
The main subject of this poem is the "old farmhouse" mentioned in the title and in line 2.

Incorrect choices:

A A man and his wife are mentioned in the sixth stanza, but they are not the subject of the poem.

B The house is located on the road to Suffern, but the road is not the subject.

D A gang of workmen is mentioned in the fourth stanza, but this is not the subject of the poem.

14. Correct response: **B**
(*Analyze literary elements: theme*)
The sixth stanza in particular expresses this idea that houses become "human."

Incorrect choices:

A The speaker suggests that houses should have families in them, not just babies or not necessarily babies.

C The speaker wants to fix up the old house, not take it down.

D The speaker likes to see houses well kept, but the most important thing is to have someone living in the house.

15. Correct response: **B**
(*Identify literary devices*)
The speaker compares a new but empty house to "a hat on its block in the store." Both are new and perfectly nice, but they have no "personality" yet because they have not been used.

Incorrect choices:

A The speaker associates an old, empty house with a broken heart (line 29).

C The speaker mentions the "loving wooden arms" of a house (line 23) but does not compare them to a new, empty house.

D The speaker mentions vines that should be trimmed (line 11), but these are symptoms of a house that has been neglected.

16. Correct response: **D**
(*Interpret poetry and its characteristics*)
The rhyme scheme is *aabbcc. . . .*

Incorrect choices:

A The lines of the poem do follow a regular rhythm, as you can tell if you read the poem aloud.

B This poem is more of a monologue or personal narrative; it does not contain any conversation.

C There is really only one example of repetition (in lines 1 and 26).

17. Correct response: **A**
(*Analyze literary elements: setting*)
The speaker walks "along the Erie track," as in the railroad track.

Incorrect choices:

B The poem does not reveal where the speaker lives, but the setting of the poem seems to be in the country (a farmhouse standing alone).

C There is no indication that the speaker is on an island, and most islands do not have railroads.

D There is nothing in the poem to suggest a foreign country; there's a town named Suffern in New York, and Erie is the name of a town in Pennsylvania, a canal in New York, and one of the Great Lakes.

18. Correct response: **D**
(*Make inferences and generalizations*)
The speaker feels that an empty old house has a broken heart and would like to fix it up for someone who wants a home. These things suggest someone who cares about or sympathizes with other people.

Incorrect choices:

A Even though the speaker does seem to like to walk, he doesn't express unhappiness with where he is.

B A "delight in life" doesn't fit with the poem's sad, thoughtful mood.

C The speaker may be honest, but it doesn't come up in the poem.

Don't Believe Everything You Read

19. Correct response: **C**
(*Identify main idea and supporting details*)
This main idea can be inferred from the first and last paragraphs.

19. (continued)

Incorrect choices:

A This is a detail that could be part of Mencken's false history of the tub.

B This is a generalization that does not refer to Mencken.

D This sentence mentions only Mencken and does not refer to the bathtub story.

20. Correct response: **B**

(*Identify sequence of events*)

The first paragraph indicates that Mencken wrote the story just after the United States entered World War I.

Incorrect choices:

A This event took place in 2003, many years after the article first appeared.

C The article was published just after the United States entered the war.

D Mencken told the truth in 1926, about nine years after the article came out.

21. Correct response: **D**

(*Select sources of information*)

On the Internet, you could find all sorts of information about the bathtub, including the original Mencken article.

Incorrect choices:

A Dictionaries do not provide historical information.

B Television could give you some useful information, but only if you happened to find a program about the bathtub.

C A book of world records might have something related to bathtubs but the rest of the history wouldn't be in it.

22. Correct response: **A**

(*Use etymology, root words, and word origins to determine word meaning*)

The word *legal* refers to law, and *il-* is a negative prefix meaning "not or against."

Incorrect choices:

B, C, and **D** are plausible choices, but none gives the meaning of *illegal*.

23. Correct response: **C**

(*Draw conclusions*)

The passage says that Mencken wrote the article because he wanted to "give Americans a good chuckle," or make them laugh, and he thought they would enjoy it.

Incorrect choices:

A Mencken may have embarrassed some readers, but this was not his reason for writing the article.

B He clarified the facts in 1926, but he made up the "facts" in his article.

D He wrote the article to entertain people, not to educate them.

24. Correct response: **A**

(*Use text features*)

This idea can be inferred from the title's telling people not to believe everything they read.

Incorrect choices:

B The title warns people not to believe *everything* they read, but it does not suggest that the facts in *most* news articles are wrong.

C The title suggests that readers should question the truth of everything, including articles they find on the Internet.

D Mencken may have caused some problems with his article, but the title does not suggest that they were serious.

25. Correct response: **D**
(*Make connections*)
 A story on Bigfoot with a fake photo is most like Mencken's article because it is made up and not true.

Incorrect choices:

A and **C** are examples of factual articles that give true information.

B An essay gives the writer's personal opinions or an argument, but this is not an article with false information made up by the writer to entertain readers.

A Meeting at Dawn

26. Correct response: **C**
(*Identify literary genres and their characteristics*)
 This story is set in 1599, it includes historical details, and the characters could have been real people.

Incorrect choices:

A Folktales are set in the past, but they usually have something unrealistic about them, such as magical spells or talking animals.

B An informational article does not include characters or dialogue.

D A biography tells the life story of a real person.

27. Correct response: **C**
(*Use details or evidence from the text to support ideas*)
 The fact that the tribes trade with one another indicates that they are not fighting.

Incorrect choices:

A The passage doesn't say it's a common food.

B The arrival of guns and horses does not indicate that the tribes get along.

D This detail shows only that there is no fighting at the market because the soldiers keep the peace.

28. Correct response: **A**
(*Make inferences*)
 Tohono's father was too surprised to say more than "*Buenos días*" (good day) when the priests greeted them in a friendly way, and Tohono wondered, "What kind of Spaniards are these?"

Incorrect choices:

B The narrator clearly understands the word *amigos*—and his father probably does, too—because he says that the priest "actually sounded like he did consider us friends."

C Tohono and his father go to Cicuye often on market days and are used to seeing many other people.

D The story suggests that the Spanish are not very friendly, but it does not suggest that other Indians behave in unfriendly ways.

29. Correct response: **D**
(*Analyze literary elements: narrative point of view*)
 The last paragraph reveals that the narrator, some years after the event, is telling about something that happened when he was a boy.

Incorrect choices:

A The narrator meets Father Martinez on the road and refers to him by name.

B The narrator tells the story in the first person ("I," "my father," and so on) as a participant, so he can't be an outside observer.

C The narrator's father is a Tewa, so he cannot be a Spanish soldier.

30. Correct response: **B**
(*Use context clues to determine word meaning*)
 Since it's early morning and they are having trouble seeing the travelers, there must not be enough light.

30. (continued)
Incorrect choices:

A The word *meager* refers to the light, not the two men.

C The word *meager* could refer to supplies, but in this case it refers to the light.

D This meaning is contradicted by the fact that they can't see clearly.

31. Correct response: **C**
(*Recognize author's style, tone, mood*)
The narrator is fondly recalling an important day from his youth, so the story's mood is reflective, or thoughtful.

Incorrect choices:

A The narrator may have reason to be sad about events in his past, but he doesn't express those feelings in the story.

B Characters in the story laugh, but the general mood isn't lighthearted.

D The narrator is surprised and pleased by how friendly the priests are, so the mood isn't angry or resentful.

32. Correct response: **A**
(*Make inferences*)
They were friendly to Tohono and his father, and they warmly "greeted every new face" on the way to the market.

Incorrect choices:

B The missionaries are happy to meet new people and don't seem very worried about possibly dangerous wild pigs.

C They don't seem very tired, despite their hard journey and lack of sleep.

D There is no evidence in the passage that the missionaries plan to take over anything.

Wangari Maathai: Better Living Through Trees and The Nobel Peace Prize

33. Correct response: **B**
(*Distinguish fact and opinion*)
This sentence states a fact that can be verified.

Incorrect choices:

A This sentence expresses Dr. Maathai's husband's opinion of her and cannot be proven true.

C and D are Dr. Maathai's opinions and cannot be proven true.

34. Correct response: **C**
(*Identify main idea and supporting details*)
This sentence best sums up Dr. Maathai's view that when the land and people's lives have improved, peace will follow.

Incorrect choices:

A People are paid to plant trees, but this is only one small benefit.

B Trees help to feed animals, but this does not make their owners feel more peaceful.

D People who plant trees may become tired, but this does not lead to peace.

35. Correct response: **D**
(*Draw conclusions*)
Her environmental work demonstrates that she believes people must share Earth with other forms of life.

Incorrect choices:

A Dr. Maathai thinks trees are important, but nothing in the passage indicates that she thinks they are more important than other plants.

B Dr. Maathai has opposed her government and has been punished for it, so she would not agree with this statement.

C Dr. Maathai does not work at home, and she believes that women "must free themselves from silence and fear."

36. Correct response: **A**
(*Compare and contrast*)
The seventh paragraph says, "Unlike most African women, she went to school," and she was the first Kenyan woman ever to earn a doctorate.

Incorrect choices:

B Most other women probably have opinions about the government, too, even if they don't speak out.

C Most if not all women care about natural resources, too; more than 50,000 women in the Green Belt Movement have planted trees.

D Getting married and having a family does not make Dr. Maathai different from other women.

37. Correct response: **B**
(*Evaluate author's purpose*)
The author wrote this biographical passage to give information about Dr. Wangari Maathai.

Incorrect choices:

A The author wrote this passage to inform readers, not to persuade.

C This passage was not written as a story to entertain.

D The author tells how Dr. Maathai started the Green Belt Movement, but explaining its history is not the main purpose of the passage.

38. Correct response: **C**
(*Use graphic features: chart*)
The chart of Nobel Peace Prize winners indicates that Mohamed ElBaradei is from Egypt.

Incorrect choices:

A Kofi Annan is from Ghana, not Egypt.

B Shirin Ebadi is from Iran, not Egypt.

D Maathai is from Kenya, not Egypt.

39. Correct response: **A**
(*Use context clues to determine word meaning*)
The second paragraph explains that Nobel was a *philanthropist* who gave money to a fund and wanted to help people improve their lives.

Incorrect choices:

B The prizes are now given out by an organization, but that is not the meaning of *philanthropist*.

C A *philanthropist* can give money for many causes, not just the environment.

D A *philanthropist* is a kind of leader, but he or she is not elected and does not usually work for the government.

40. Correct response: **D**
(*Make connections*)
Both passages tell about the Nobel Peace Prize; Passage 1 tells about a person who won it.

Incorrect choices:

A Planting trees is discussed only in Passage 1.

B The Green Belt Movement is discussed only in Passage 1.

C Global warming is not a focus of either passage.

1. B	**11.** D	**21.** C	**31.** C
2. B	**12.** A	**22.** D	**32.** D
3. D	**13.** D	**23.** A	**33.** B
4. C	**14.** A	**24.** D	**34.** C
5. C	**15.** D	**25.** B	**35.** B
6. A	**16.** C	**26.** A	**36.** C
7. B	**17.** C	**27.** D	**37.** A
8. D	**18.** B	**28.** C	**38.** D
9. A	**19.** C	**29.** A	**39.** C
10. B	**20.** B	**30.** A	**40.** B

Answer Key Explanations

The Goat Well

1. Correct response: **B**
(*Recognize author's style, tone, mood*)
   Saying that someone is "not quite honest" is a witty or amusing way of saying he is dishonest.

Incorrect choices:

A and **C** are incorrect. The story is told with a sense of amusement, not sadness or anger.

D The tone of the story is one of amusement, not seriousness.

2. Correct response: **B**
(*Interpret figurative language, including idioms*)
   "Adding insult to injury" is an idiom. The thirsty man found that the well was dry, and that was bad enough; then his goat fell into the well and made the whole situation even worse.

2. (continued)
Incorrect choices:

A and **D** are possible interpretations, but neither one fits the meaning of the phrase.

C This is a literal interpretation of the idiom.

3. Correct response: **D**
(*Make inferences*)
   The passage says the man was "quick-witted" when he replied to the trader's request for a drink, and right away he said the well was a goat well. These two clues show that the man knew he could profit from the well when the man asked for a drink.

Incorrect choices:

A This did not actually happen; the scoundrel made it up to impress the trader.

B The scoundrel was by himself when the goat fell in so he did not yet see a way to profit from the well.

C When the trader began to bargain, the scoundrel had practically closed the deal.

4. Correct response: **C**
(*Analyze characters*)

Despite his initial disbelief, the trader was easily fooled because he accepted the story that the well produced goats.

Incorrect choices:

A The trader is not clever enough to avoid being fooled and trading everything he has for a dry well.

B The trader may be greedy to some extent, but not overly so; he is a trader trying to make a profit.

D The trader is not completely honest himself; he reveals only enough information to make the deal and then later to locate the scoundrel.

5. Correct response: **C**
(*Use context clues to determine the meaning of multiple-meaning words*)

The phrase "cunning scoundrel" gives a clue that there is some trickery going on as the scoundrel introduces the idea of a sale into the trader's mind.

Incorrect choices:

A, **B**, and **D** are all meanings of the word *plant*, but none of them fits in the context of this sentence.

6. Correct response: **A**
(*Analyze literary elements: theme*)

The key to the theme is at the end of the story when the cheater is found, forced to return his ill-gotten goods, and publicly punished.

6. (continued)
Incorrect choices:

B Being wary of strangers is probably a good idea, but that is not the theme of this story.

C The scoundrel pretends that the well is magic, but the existence of magic is not the theme of the story.

D This theme does not fit the story, since both men made mistakes and both paid for them in different ways.

More Travel, Smarter People?

7. Correct response: **B**
(*Identify main idea and supporting details*)

Mead's main point is that people who travel are wiser than those who never leave home.

Incorrect choices:

A People who travel do spend money, but this is not Mead's point.

C Some people travel to go to school, but traveling does not cause people to enroll in better schools.

D People who travel may earn higher salaries, but this was not Mead's point.

8. Correct response: **D**
(*Identify main idea and supporting details*)

The main focus of this passage is traveling to other countries, and the main statistic is "international arrivals."

Incorrect choices:

A Business travel is included in the circle graph, but it is not the focus of the passage.

B Travel to the United States is discussed in paragraphs 4 and 5, but this is not the focus of the passage.

C Automobile travel is mentioned in the passage, but this is not the main focus.

9. Correct response: **A**
(*Interpret graphic features: graphs*)
   Russia had the fewest visitors in 2006 (about 20 million), as shown in the bar graph.

Incorrect choices:

B, **C**, and **D** are incorrect. All of these countries had more visitors than Russia did.

10. Correct response: **B**
(*Interpret graphic features: graphs*)
   The circle graph (or pie chart) shows that the greatest number of U.S. travelers (43 percent) visited other countries for vacation/fun, or "pleasure."

Incorrect choices:

A About 21 percent of U.S. travelers went for business or work.

C and **D** are incorrect. Only about 2 percent of U.S. travelers go for a conference or to study or teach.

11. Correct response: **D**
(*Use context clues to determine meaning of unfamiliar words*)
   The word *overseas* is used interchangeably with the word *abroad* in the text and in the title of the circle graph, so *abroad* must mean "out of one's own country."

Incorrect choices:

A Traveling abroad may involve a great distance, but that is not what the word means.

B People may travel several times, but that is not the meaning of the word.

C People may travel to more than one place, but that is not the meaning of the word.

12. Correct response: **A**
(*Make predictions*)
   Since the World Tourism Organization reports that more people travel out of their own country every year, the best prediction is that there will be more travel next year than this year.

Incorrect choices:

B The passage says that air travel is growing, but it gives no specific information about travel by car.

C The passage says that the number of travelers keeps growing every year, so the number next year will probably not be the same as this year.

D There isn't any information in the passage to support this prediction.

Joey Solves the Problem

13. Correct response: **D**
(*Identify literary genres and their characteristics*)
   The story has realistic characters and could happen in real life, so it is realistic fiction.

Incorrect choices:

A A fantasy includes characters or places that could not exist in real life.

B An informational article is factual and does not have characters.

C A folktale generally takes place long ago, has standard kinds of characters (such as the farmer or the fisherman), and often has some form of magical being in it.

14. Correct response: **A**
(*Identify cause and effect*)
   Dad didn't hire the pest control company because the job would cost hundreds of dollars.

14. (continued)

Incorrect choices:

B The company would guarantee its work, but only if a wire fence was installed.

C He was less concerned about the lawn than about the cost.

D He hoped the skunk would leave on its own because he could not afford to have it removed.

15. Correct response: **D**
(*Make inferences*)
You can tell from what she says ("If that skunk doesn't move out, I'm going to!") that the skunk problem really bothers her.

Incorrect choices:

A She wants to trap the skunk or get rid of it in any way they can.

B Joey uses the computer, but the story gives no reason to think that computers make Mom nervous.

C The story says that Mom goes off to work, but there is no evidence that she does not like her job.

16. Correct response: **C**
(*Identify sequence of events*)
Joey turned on the porch light after he learned online that skunks dislike bright light.

Incorrect choices:

A Dad talked to the pest-control people before Joey got home.

B Joey learned about skunks that night after he and Mom both got home.

D The skunk sprayed again on the first night, before Joey learned about skunks.

17. Correct response: **C**
(*Use prefixes and suffixes to determine word meaning*)
The suffix -*ist*, meaning "one who," combines with the word *special* to mean "one who has special knowledge."

Incorrect choices:

A This meaning would fit an adverb, such as *specially*.

B This meaning would fit a word with a noun suffix (such as -*ness* or -*hood*).

D This meaning would need a negative prefix, such as *non-* or *un-*.

18. Correct response: **B**
(*Make predictions*)
Dad says that if Joey's idea works, they will buy the new computer he's been wishing for.

Incorrect choices:

A The skunk has been driven out by the ammonia and is not likely to return with babies.

C Mom threatened to move out if the skunk problem was not solved, but then it was solved.

D The story ends in the morning when Joey wakes up, so he will probably not go back to sleep until that night.

Astronaut Visits Hometown

19. Correct response: **C**
(*Evaluate author's purpose*)
The author wrote this passage to give information about Sunita Williams.

19. (continued)
Incorrect choices:

A This passage is informational, not persuasive.

B The passage tells about Williams but does not compare her with others.

D This passage is not written as a story to entertain.

20. Correct response: **B**
(*Distinguish fact and opinion*)
   This statement is a personal view that cannot be verified as fact.

Incorrect choices:

A, **C**, and **D** all state facts that can be proven true.

21. Correct response: **C**
(*Summarize*)
   This sentence best summarizes what the paragraph is mainly about.

Incorrect choices:

A This sentence is a generalization that does not summarize the important points in the paragraph.

B This sentence gives only one detail, which refers back to the fourth paragraph.

D This is an opinion that does not summarize the important points in the paragraph.

22. Correct response: **D**
(*Use details or evidence from the text to support ideas*)
   Exchanging e-mail with young students is the only answer that involves someone other than Sunita herself, so it supports the idea that she helps others.

22. (continued)
Incorrect choices:

A, **B**, and **C** all tell about Williams's hard work and what she has accomplished herself.

23. Correct response: **A**
(*Interpret figurative language, including idioms*)
   The passage says that the students have set exercise goals for themselves, so they have clearly been affected by Williams's own fitness program and have taken her ideas seriously.

Incorrect choices:

B, **C**, and **D** are plausible answers, but none fits the meaning of the phrase.

24. Correct response: **D**
(*Use context clues to determine the meaning of multiple-meaning words*)
   She *logged the most time* means that she "traveled for a certain distance or time."

Incorrect choices:

A, **B**, and **C** do not fit the context of the sentence, especially definitions 1 and 2 because they refer to the word *log* as a noun instead of a verb.

25. Correct response: **B**
(*Select sources of information*)
   Since Williams was an astronaut for NASA, the best, most up-to-date resource would be the NASA Web site.

Incorrect choices:

A An encyclopedia would probably not be current enough to include this information and would not be this specific about one astronaut's experiences.

C The almanac would list Williams and her flights as an astronaut but would not give much information about her work on the space station.

D A thesaurus gives synonyms and antonyms, not information about people or events.

Fair Payment

26. Correct response: **A**
(*Identify literary genres and their characteristics*)
Folktales typically begin with a phrase such as "Long ago" or " Once upon a time."

Incorrect choices:

B Characters can have a disagreement in any kind of fiction or drama.

C The action taking place in one day is not an essential or unique characteristic of a folktale.

D Characters may speak in any kind of fiction or drama, not just folktales.

27. Correct response: **D**
(*Distinguish denotative and connotative meanings*)
The word *aroma* refers to an odor or smell and usually describes a smell that is pleasant or appetizing, such as the smell of cooking food.

Incorrect choices:

A, **B**, and **C** are plausible answers, but they do not fit the meaning or the connotation of *aroma*.

28. Correct response: **C**
(*Identify cause and effect*)
The third paragraph says that Luke held the bread over the kettle so the bread could "absorb the flavor of the rising steam."

Incorrect choices:

A Luke did not have any reason to change the color of the bread.

B Steam might clean the bread, but that is not why Luke held his bread over the kettle.

D He could have warmed the bread with steam, but steam would not bake the bread.

29. Correct response: **A**
(*Analyze characters*)
The second paragraph describes the baker as "softhearted," says that he "took pity" on Luke, and tells how he offered Luke a thick slice of bread.

Incorrect choices:

B Luke was honest and forthright, but he did not do anything kind or generous.

C The cook was not kind or generous, as he tried to charge Luke for taking his steam.

D The king was fair and shrewd, but he did not do anything kind or generous.

30. Correct response: **A**
(*Make connections*)
In this story, the cook demands payment for the steam that rises from his stew, although it is of no use to him. This is most similar to a brother who gets upset with his sister for playing with a toy when he isn't using it.

Incorrect choices:

B, **C**, and **D** are incorrect. In all of these situations, a brother and sister argue over something that both of them want but only one can have—unlike the cook and Luke, who argue over something that neither one can possess.

31. Correct response: **C**
(*Make inferences*)
The cook smiled smugly at Luke because he expected real payment, so he must have been shocked and disappointed by the king's decision.

Incorrect choices:

A The cook did not seem timid or afraid at any time in the story.

B Luke might have been amused and relieved, but the cook was not.

D The cook was not happy or grateful because he got no actual payment.

32. Correct response: **D**
(*Analyze literary elements: theme*)
    The cook made a huge fuss over some steam, which would have evaporated anyway, and got nothing for all his trouble.

Incorrect choices:

A Luke, the king, and the cook all expressed their opinions to make their cases, so this lesson does not fit the story.

B This may be true of the king, but it does not explain a lesson the story teaches.

C None of the characters was actually a thief, so this lesson does not fit the story.

Titanic Troubles and Undersea Explorer

33. Correct response: **B**
(*Use context clues to determine word meaning*)
    Leaving a loved one behind on a sinking ship would have to be an emotional experience.

Incorrect choices:

A, **C**, and **D** could fit into the sentence grammatically, but they do not fit the context or the meaning of *poignant*.

34. Correct response: **C**
(*Identify main idea and supporting details*)
    This sentence from the second paragraph supports the idea that only experts using the best equipment could find the *Titanic* because its location was unknown and it had been missing for 73 years.

Incorrect choices:

A This description of the *Titanic* does not relate to the difficulty of finding it.

B This description of what happened does not relate to the difficulty of finding it.

D This sentence tells what Ballard decided but not how difficult the search would be.

35. Correct response: **B**
(*Evaluate author's point of view*)
    In the fifth paragraph, the author states, "Sadly, tourism has been bad for the *Titanic*." This statement reveals the author's view that tourists should treat the site with more respect.

Incorrect choices:

A The author seems fascinated by the *Titanic* and does not suggest that seeing it would be a waste of money.

C The author does not imply that tourists are sure to enjoy their trip.

D The author refers to explorers as brave and adventurous, but not the tourists.

36. Correct response: **C**
(*Identify text structure/organization*)
    The passage presents information in chronological order, from the sinking of the *Titanic* in 1912 to its discovery in 1985 to today.

Incorrect choices:

A, **B**, and **D** are other ways to organize information, but they do not describe the structure of this passage.

37. Correct response: **A**
(*Select sources of information*)
    Additional details about the *Titanic* and its voyage can be found in an encyclopedia.

Incorrect choices:

B A dictionary does not provide detailed historical information about events.

C An atlas is a book of maps and does not usually provide historical information.

D A thesaurus provides synonyms and antonyms, not historical information.

38. Correct response: **D**

(*Summarize*)

This is the best summary of the passage, which gives information about Ballard's entire life, his career, and his discovery of the *Titanic* and other ships.

Incorrect choices:

A This answer focuses on Ballard's early years and does not mention the *Titanic*.

B This answer mentions some unimportant details that should be omitted from a summary.

C This answer focuses on Ballard today and omits both his early years and his discovery of the *Titanic*.

39. Correct response: **C**

(*Identify sequence of events*)

Both passages explain that Ballard developed special unmanned vehicles in the 1980s that enabled him to find the *Titanic*.

Incorrect choices:

A, **B**, and **D** are incorrect. Passage 2 says that Ballard studied underwater mountains, discovered sea animals, and predicted volcanoes under the ocean while he was working at Woods Hole in the 1970s, so he did all of these things before he developed unmanned vehicles and began searching for the *Titanic*.

40. Correct response: **B**

(*Make connections*)

Both passages describe discoveries that Robert Ballard has made.

Incorrect choices:

A This information is discussed only in Passage 1.

C The *Bismarck* and the *U.S.S. Yorktown* are mentioned only in Passage 2.

D The fact that Ballard took pictures of *Titanic* is mentioned only in Passage 1.

Standardized Test Tutor: Reading

Student Scoring Chart

Grade **6**

Student Name _____

Teacher Name _____

Test 1	Item Numbers	Number Correct/Total	Percent (%)
"A Tough Decision" (realistic fiction)	1–6	/6	
"Where Have All the Chestnuts Gone?" (informational)	7–12	/6	
"At the Aquarium" and "In March" (poems)	13–18	/6	
"A Story of Hope" (informational)	19–25	/7	
"The Silver Mouse" (folktale)	26–32	/7	
"So You Want to Donate Blood" and "Student Council Holds Blood Drive" (informational)	33–40	/8	
Total	**1–40**	**/40**	

Test 2	Item Numbers	Number Correct/Total	Percent (%)
"The Bridge of the Gods" (myth)	1–6	/6	
"Wondrous, Dangerous Plastic" (informational)	7–12	/6	
"The House With Nobody in It" (poem)	13–18	/6	
"Don't Believe Everything You Read" (informational)	19–25	/7	
"A Meeting at Dawn" (historical fiction)	26–32	/7	
"Wangari Maathai: Better Living Through Trees" and "The Nobel Peace Prize" (informational)	33–40	/8	
Total	**1–40**	**/40**	

Test 3	Item Numbers	Number Correct/Total	Percent (%)
"The Goat Well" (folktale)	1–6	/6	
"More Travel, Smarter People?" (informational)	7–12	/6	
"Joey Solves the Problem" (realistic fiction)	13–18	/6	
"Astronaut Visits Hometown" (news article)	19–25	/7	
"Fair Payment" (folktale)	26–32	/7	
"Titanic Troubles" and "Undersea Explorer" (informational)	33–40	/8	
Total	**1–40**	**/40**	

Standardized Test Tutor: Reading

Classroom Scoring Chart

Teacher Name _____

Student Name	Test 1	Test 2	Test 3

Notes:

Notes: